C000199555

'I found Sandra's book a f[...] work as a missionary nurs[...] days before mobile phone[...] resilience as she faces dif[...] journeys almost daily. As a former missionary nurse in rural Congo in the same era, my life seemed easy! It was breathtaking to read about some of her hair-raising journeys.

'All through the book we are given an honest insight into her ongoing discipleship journey. Too often missionaries feel they have been put on a pedestal, yet they face the same everyday temptations as anyone anywhere else in the world.

'Interwoven with the storyline, Sandra quietly teaches us more about our loving heavenly Father who will never leave us or forsake us and who provides for our needs as we trust in Him. I found this book very encouraging and helpful. Even the appendix about coping with different cultural values is clear and helpful for living in our complex multicultural society.'
Mary Weeks Millard, former missionary nurse, author of *Belle of the Ball*

'In her autobiography, Sandra Michie has shown what it means to seek and to follow God's plan for your life. The early years are full of uncertainties about whether to live in Africa or the UK, what training to have, which missionary society would be best for her, how to raise finance, how to cope with travelling on rudimentary roads and shaky river crossings, how to live without basic amenities that are enjoyed in Europe, how to communicate with the local people in Zambia.

'It is a story full of adventure and unexpected events set in a remote part of Zambia where her medical skills were tested in primitive conditions as she coped with all kinds of emergencies and local superstitions. Her faith in God's guidance and provision shines through in the narrative, which continues on through her eventual return to the UK and up to the present day. The book will encourage and be an inspiration to all who feel uncertain about their security in the Lord.'

Derek Butters, former chairman of The Evangelization Society (TES)

'I have very much enjoyed reading Sandra's book, *God's Patchwork*. I love her honesty and willingness to recount her life experiences in a transparent way. I was greatly impressed by Sandra when I worked with her at Lukolwe. She has a genuine love for the Luvale people and, as well as having a fluency in the language, her relationship with them was one of warmth and mutual respect. Her leadership and medical skills were extraordinary.

'In 2018 God enabled Sandra and me to visit Lukolwe after more than a quarter of a century. During our brief visit there was an outpouring of love showered upon Sandra that was a delight to behold.'

Nicki Hunt (née Keen), former missionary nurse colleague and friend

To Hazel,
    Happy Birthday!
With love & blessings,
        Zillah.

7-12-18

God's Patchwork

*Stories of a missionary nurse
in rural Zambia*

Sandra Michie

instant
apostle

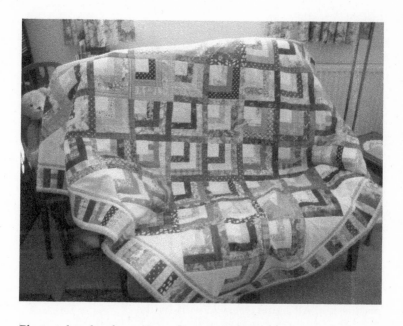

Photo taken by the author of own patchwork quilt made herself from scrap materials

First published in Great Britain in 2018

Instant Apostle
The Barn
1 Watford House Lane
Watford
Herts
WD17 1BJ

Copyright © Sandra Michie 2018

if notified, will formally seek permission at the earliest opportunity.

The views and opinions expressed in this work are those of the author and do not necessarily reflect the views and opinions of the publisher.

Some names have been changed to protect anonymity.

British Library Cataloguing-in-Publication Data

A catalogue record for this book is available from the British Library

This book and all other Instant Apostle books are available from Instant Apostle:

Website: www.instantapostle.com

E-mail: info@instantapostle.com

ISBN 978-1-909728-93-6

Printed and bound in Great Britain by Clays Ltd, Elcograf S.p.A.

Dedication

Through the years so many people have touched my life in countless ways. It has been a deliberate choice not to try to name the vast majority of you as it would be impossible to cover everyone. Those who are named are the ones who are very much part of the story as presented here, but I am conscious that the rich patchwork of my life has been touched and changed by myriad others. For each one of you I am so grateful for what God has done through you.

This book is dedicated to each person God has used
to make me someone He could use.

Contents

Introduction

One morning I was listening to *Thought for the Day* on the radio when the comment was made that every person has a unique story and ...'Out of this came ME'.[1] So this is a personal story about a unique person, moulded, led and blended by an utterly unique God.

Patchwork is made by taking all sorts of disparate pieces and combining them into a thing of beauty. In the process only the designer can envisage the completed article. Hindsight is marvellous. It can change how we see and understand things and allows us greater appreciation of the whole. Looking back over a long life, I am amazed to realise something of the pattern that has formed from apparently unrelated pieces. Perhaps most of all is the wonder in realising how through each stage of life I had been prepared for what was to come in the years ahead. And there is more to come.

This story has been written after encouragement from many other people, and I am so grateful to them all. In

---

[1] A comment heard and noted one morning around 2014, from *Thought for the Day* on BBC Radio 4; no accurate record of the date or speaker.

writing it I have learned anew much of God's planning in love for his children.

> For we are God's handiwork, created in Christ
> Jesus to do good works, which God prepared in
> advance for us to do.
> (Ephesians 2:10)

Our pontoon on the Zambezi River, with my Toyota Land Cruiser on board. Myself with the designer and builder of the pontoon and some local folk.
Image courtesy of Nicki Hunt, used with permission.

Zambezi River

After two hard days of driving the fully laden Land Cruiser and trailer over rough dirt roads from the nearest town, we finally reached the banks of the mighty Zambezi River. We were nearly home. Our destination was only ten miles away, across the river which had no bridges.

One of our team had built a Heath Robinson pontoon for crossing the river. It was constructed from a frame made of welded piping holding empty forty-four-gallon fuel drums for buoyancy. With ramps on either end, we had to drive the vehicle up and onto the two narrow wooden strips across the surface of the pontoon. The fibreglass boat with outboard engine was then tied to the side and used to push the whole contraption across the river. It was basic, it looked crude, but it worked.

It was flood season, so the river was wide, very deep and with a strong current. There was only myself as driver, and two workmen to assist in controlling the pontoon. The pickup had half a ton of essential food and medical supplies on board. The huge trailer carried another ton, mainly drums of fuel (petrol, diesel and paraffin), but the pontoon was built to take such a load. Putting the Land Cruiser into low-range four-wheel drive was a routine safety measure.

As I drove up the ramps, the ropes securing it to the riverbank slipped from their moorings and released the whole pontoon. The weight of the load and heavy trailer pushed it out into the river away from the supporting bank. The trailer was still on the ramp, resulting in everything beginning to tip, threatening to empty us backwards into the flooded river. Gunning the accelerator, the wheels gripped and climbed the 'mountain' ahead (perhaps a 45-degree angle, although it felt like more) and eventually the whole combination levelled out again. Slamming on the brakes to prevent the Land Cruiser rolling off the other end, I discovered that the vehicle and I had floated right out into the middle of the river and were beginning to drift downstream in the current.

Trembling, I managed to climb out of the vehicle, push blocks in front of the wheels for safety and scramble over the framework into the attached boat. Thankfully, the outboard motor started easily and enabled the whole assembly to be driven back towards the bank. The two terrified workmen were waiting, knowing they had failed to control the pontoon and having been watching as the vehicle appeared to slide backwards off the ramp and towards the deep water. They had been convinced that both vehicle and driver were going to end up at the bottom of the crocodile-infested river!

Truth be told, so had I! But instinctive responses had kicked in and it was only afterwards that the full realisation of the danger hit me. It was after reaching home some ninety minutes later that the shaking really started and it took some time before the resulting nightmares stopped.

Travel in our isolated area of Zambia was never easy.

LOOKING BACK

By the time of that particular river crossing I had been living and working in that remote north-western corner of Zambia for several years. The story of how I went there was a long episode in the patchwork of my life, which began just as an unexpected bomb was dropped outside the hospital in Dartford, probably in error. It was 7th September 1940 and the first bombing wave of the London Blitz. After more than four years of marriage and numerous treatments, my mother had been told that she would never conceive her own child and my parents had been accepted on to the list to adopt a baby. Then war broke out. A doctor's visit resulted in the comment, 'Well, if I did not know better I would say you were pregnant.' By the September of that year an overdose of Victoria plums apparently sent my mother into labour. Thankfully, life continued at a less startling rate.

War, with my father's work managing an aircraft factory in Durham, moved us up to Keighley in Yorkshire and we spent much of the next seven years there before emigrating, initially to South Africa, and later travelling further northwards to

Rhodesia. My memories of those first ten years of my life were sparse, but during high-school years in Bulawayo and then in Salisbury, Rhodesia, I learned to love that country and it felt like home.

Emigration

All through childhood and teenage years I did not feel important in our family. That was probably not true of my dad's attitude, but with the blanket vision of remembered childhood, it felt like that. More recently I have been challenged on that belief.

It was a Monday in July 2009 when a visit to the chest clinic at Harefield Hospital left me rather shaken at the diagnosis of bronchiectasis. The consultant had been very thorough in his questioning and had taken me right back to childhood, asking about chest infections. It stirred my memory of how, according to comments made by my parents, in the very severe winter of early 1947 I had been extremely ill twice with 'double pneumonia' and left with a primary tuberculosis (TB) 'spot on the lung'. The doctor's only advice at that time, when there were no drugs yet generally available to treat TB,[2] was to 'take this child out to a warm climate'. I had known that this had been an influencing factor in my parents' decision to emigrate to South Africa, but it was only after that 2009

---

[2] https://en.wikipedia.org/wiki/History_of_tuberculosis#Twentieth_cen tury (accessed 24th April 2018).

diagnosis that timing and actions came together in my mind and I began to realise what they had been willing to sacrifice for my health. I checked this out with my brother who confirmed his understanding of the story.

My dad's younger brother married in September 1947 and he and his wife moved in with Grandma Michie, caring for her. Then Grandpa Crockett (Mum's father) died in November and his wife went to Canada to live with her son and family, so another responsibility was eased. This paved the way for us, as a small family, to emigrate to South Africa. By Christmas of 1947 my father was on his way to Johannesburg to look for work and a place to stay. The rest of us travelled the following April. I lived in different parts of Africa for most of the next forty-two years; my brother and family are still there and my parents remained in Rhodesia, now Zimbabwe, for the rest of their lives. It was not only a health-changing but also a life-changing choice to emigrate.

Image courtesy of iancoombe.tripod.com (accessed 2nd April 2013).

The journey out there could not have been easy and almost certainly was by way of the £10 assisted post-war passages available at that time to South Africa, Australia, New Zealand and Canada.[3] Dad left Southampton on the *Carnarvon Castle* on 16th December 1947 and the rest of us travelled on the *Winchester Castle* leaving on 6th April 1948, after he had found a job to support the family. The Union-Castle Line ships were still in their wartime troopship layout with huge cabins lined with many bunks, three deep on all sides. The *Winchester Castle* was built to carry 487 passengers and had 890 on board for that journey.[4] Parents were warned to care for their own children, as the decks only had strands of cable running around the edges and a child could easily slip underneath and fall overboard. The stewards (one of whom was my father's cousin) took my brother, aged four, and dressed him up for the fancy-dress party on board. He was clad in old torn dungarees, with a toothbrush and so on hanging around his neck. An address label stated 'Austerity passenger'. To their delight he won first prize.

Another memory is of landing in Cape Town and Dad meeting us on the dock. He then led us past some market stalls. Coming from post-war England, the fruit was beyond belief and, when asked if she would like some bananas, Mum's reply was to wonder if we could afford one to share between the four of us. In England bananas

---

[3] https://www.exodus2013.co.uk/empire-settlement-schemes-after-wwi/ accessed 24th April 2018.
[4] Details referenced from the Passenger Lists shown in www.findmypast.co.uk – accessed through a purchased subscription 29th September 2005.

were a very special treat indeed, so perhaps you can you picture her amazement when Dad bought a whole hand of them and we had two each!

Childhood in another land

Emigrating to South Africa meant a new land, but not an easy one. We lived in a 'boarding house' in the Johannesburg area. Probably within the first year, my father had the retinas of both eyes detach, followed by a major car accident, and was in hospital for many months. For my mother it must have been a nightmare.

After a time in various boarding houses we finally had a rented house in Primrose Hill, near Germiston. But for my parents, life was still very stressful. They both worked long hours. In those years, alcohol flowed freely at home and at different times the stress resulted in rows fuelled by it. One evening, after a shouting match between my parents, I can remember being locked out on the veranda of our house beside my very angry mother, but such times were rare. School was just a few blocks down the road, so my brother and I could walk there on our own. With my mother working it often meant having a door key to get into the empty house after school.

Then came the joy of a newly built home in Lombardy East. That year at Fairmount School will always be tied together in my mind with King George VI's death in 1952 and the accession of Queen Elizabeth II to the throne. The time of silence to honour the king during the school assembly on the morning of his death left an indelible impression on me. At the start of the following year, I moved up to secondary school with others from my class and, for the first and only time, felt part of the crowd. It is a lonely place, moving into a new school mid-year, and I had already been to five different primary schools since moving to South Africa.

Seven months later we were again on the move, up to Rhodesia. It was the time of the Rhodes Centenary Exhibition in 1953 and Bulawayo was overflowing with visitors. No accommodation was available. Dad had already built us a caravan, which became our main holiday accommodation. In Bulawayo my parents lived in the caravan, while they boarded my brother, David, and myself out on a farm. The owner of the farm was one of the teachers at David's school, so it proved quite convenient. We progressed from that arrangement into a rented house and finally into a new-build in Waterford, a few miles out of town. Thankfully, each place was within reasonable distance so we did not have to change schools again.

Life was lived outdoors. As children, we were free to roam, riding our bicycles wherever we wished, including to and from school. In the holidays we were able to be outdoors all day and I cannot remember there even being checks as to where we went. Life seemed safe and happy. Houses in that part of the world were almost all single-storey and the word 'bungalow' never entered our conversation. They were all just 'houses'. Mostly we had spacious and often rambling buildings with plenty of grounds around the house and large covered verandas. The highly cultivated and beautiful gardens seen in England were rare, as the climate is so different in tropical Africa. There we were surrounded by big, bold, brilliantly coloured flowers, flowering trees and birds.

Three years later we were suddenly off again, leaving Bulawayo and travelling up to Salisbury. I later understood that my dad had been swindled in business to the point of bankruptcy. The next few years were far from easy financially. We stayed on a 100-acre smallholding, fourteen miles outside the city. At home we were again free to roam in the open spaces of Africa, but it also entailed another change of schools and of routine. We only had one car, so from Monday to Friday we all left home together at 6.30am and it was a good twelve hours or so later before we returned.

During those years my mother suffered severe depression, sometimes suicidal, and struggled with daily living. In those days it was just called a 'nervous breakdown'. For us children it meant living in constant wariness, as anything could trigger her angry responses. I was repeatedly made to feel as though it was my fault.

For a child, growing up as we did, one does not question the situation. There was acceptance, but it was not always easy. Today there is a greater understanding of mental health issues and of 'third culture kids', but the reality is that, besides all we gained, there was also real loss – the loss of extended family and relationships. The constant moving meant there were no deep ongoing friendships and one had to learn to 'leave it all behind'. From the ages of three to seventeen I changed schools eight times and it was often in the middle of a school year.

Gradually life settled down again, and the new business that my father started on his own thrived and grew. My parents bought twenty-five acres of land right next door to our rented accommodation. They built a house which was constructed from bricks made from the very ground on which it stood. It progressed as they could afford it and was another part in the preparation for what I was to face in the years ahead. There I learned many practical skills as I helped my dad with various tasks, including installing all the electrical wiring and fittings. It was some years later, after a visit to Cape Town, that the interior was finally completed by building the fireplace.

As new Christians, my parents began to go to church regularly, and that home became the centre for many church-based outings and hospitality. The huge hole from which the soil had been taken for brick-building eventually was developed into a delightful swimming pool enjoyed by many.

The phenomenon that people believe that big girls can cope, often with its corollary by implication that small women need extra care and protection, has bothered me for much of my life. Being tall (5'10½"), attaining my present height by the age of fourteen, and always being relatively uncoordinated, did not help. It often felt unfair to me that small women appeared to bring out the gentleness in menfolk!

In addition it seemed that if anything negative occurred I was the first one to be blamed. My mother responded to any stressful situation with anger, and it felt as though I was usually the brunt of, or blamed for, that anger. The outdoor life we lived meant that in daytime it was often possible to get out of the house and thus protect myself.

During our last year in South Africa our next-door neighbours had helped. They had a new baby and were very happy for me, as an eleven-year-old at the time, to babysit for them. With a short ladder as a stile over the fence between our two homes, it was easy to go next door. One day the mother was rushed to hospital for emergency surgery and it was just accepted that I was fit to be left alone to care for that six-month-old baby for the whole day. I felt valued and trusted.

An incident that occurred about the same time re-enforced the conviction that I was not important. My mother had spent two weeks in hospital after a hysterectomy and been home a few days when I set off down the road on my bicycle. She just happened to be looking out of the window and saw me slip in the sand and fall off my bike a short distance from the gate. When I failed to get up she called my dad. They rushed out of the house and the short distance to where I was lying at the side of the road.

By the time they reached me I was beginning to get up. Dazed, when they asked if I was OK the reply must have been positive. When asked why I had not stood up sooner the reply 'I didn't feel like it' (or something similar) resulted in them both venting their anger on me – Dad because he was worried about my mother, and Mum because that was her habitual way of reacting. Marched back into the house, I was sent to my room in disgrace for causing her such stress. Intermittently throughout the afternoon I was violently sick, but no one seemed to notice. That same evening they realised that something was seriously wrong and the next week was spent in hospital with concussion, having probably lost consciousness at the time of the fall. Sadly, as a child that incident subconsciously 'proved' to me that I was considered a nuisance, particularly by my mother.

This resulted in an unrecognised but deep determination not to ask for help unless it was absolutely necessary. Possibly I told myself that I had to cope because there was no one else there for me.

Accepting my physical size as the way God has made me and knowing peace about it took years, but the lack of coordination and resulting clumsiness still rears its head, particularly when fatigued or unwell. It has never helped to being told to stop being so careless! Why can some things not genuinely be an accident that needs to be accepted, without apportioning blame?

Guiding

In my teens I was considerably taller than other girls in the school and similar-aged boys of our brother school with whom we shared activities. One place where I did feel comfortable and safe was in Guiding. As a Girl Guide, my practical abilities became strengths, particularly in that outdoor life. Guiding gave me acceptance and companionship that had never been available at school. It filled some of the long afternoons (our school day finished at 1.30pm) and, having started as a Brownie, I had gone through the Guides until I was a cadet.

It also had some extra compensations for me. It was practical and became part of the preparation for those isolated years in Zambia. Before that, in July 1957, I had the privilege of being chosen as one of the eight Guides representing Southern Rhodesia at the Guide World Camp in Windsor Great Park held as a centenary tribute to Lord Baden-Powell. That camp was held for 4,000 guides from seventy different countries and was opened by the Queen.

The Guide World Camp in Windsor Great Park – 1957.
I am standing fourth from the left!

That was an interesting journey, taking three days and nights to fly in an old Avro York four-propeller plane. We travelled from Salisbury to Nairobi; on to Khartoum; then, because there was unrest in Egypt, to Benghazi (where camels meandered around the desert airstrip); over the Alps to Amsterdam and finally to London. Besides the time at the camp, we had a few weeks free for sightseeing, which allowed me to spend some time with my bedridden grandmother in Hornchurch and meet close family relatives I had not seen for almost ten years. Life in southern Africa had meant growing up with little knowledge of an extended family, so it was a new experience for me.

https://en.wikipedia.org/wiki/Avro_York#/media/File:Avro_York.jpg (accessed 18th July 18).

But there was an even greater influence at work as my Guide leader was a Christian and instrumental in my accepting Christ as Saviour. The troop was affiliated to a local evangelical Anglican church, where I also heard of God's love for me. Sometime between the ages of thirteen and fourteen I asked Jesus to come into my life, and He changed it.

In the school in Salisbury there were twin head girls in our class. They were both Christians, excited about God, and they encouraged me to go to a Crusaders group. There I began to learn more about what it meant to be a Christian. Various Scripture Union camps, Bible studies etc, including memorising the Scriptures, became part of everyday life. It was during that period I learned the value of daily spending time with God and reading His

Word – a practice I have continued ever since. Another thing learned in those days was to set aside some of my income for 'God's work'. Initially it was 10 per cent, but in later years increased to 15 per cent and even more. That habit was a choice that I have never regretted and I have often marvelled at the way that money set aside has been used through the years in blessing others and meeting real needs.

Leaving home

Thus early in my teenage years I had personally accepted the Lord Jesus Christ and the salvation He offered. As I began to understand more about the Christian life and to grow in faith, I was increasingly drawn to mission work, and read widely on the subject. At one point I even dreamt of going to China, after reading a comprehensive history of Hudson Taylor.[5]

Leaving home for further education is still a strange time for young people today. It has struck me recently how much our current young people know about the places they have chosen, having visited, from the internet, friends, etc. For me, leaving home was a step into the unknown. Cape Town was more than 2,000km (around 1,350 miles) away from where we lived and my only contact had been through the application forms completed and the limited information that came with the acceptance to train as a nurse. There was no internet, no

---

[5] Howard and Mary G Taylor, *Hudson Taylor in Early Years: The Growth of a Soul* (Philadelphia, PA: China Inland Mission, 1912), and *Hudson Taylor and the China Inland Mission: The Growth of a Work of God* (London: Morgan & Scott, 1918).

visits, and I did not even know of anyone else interested in such training.

Nursing was a natural progression of the interests shown throughout my life. I had been a carer of others for most of my childhood, and even worked in the Red Cross blood bank service as a young teenager – learning and using skills far beyond those expected from someone of such an age.

My interest in mission work had grown and after much prayer I believed that God wanted me to train as a nurse with a view to serving Him in some mission capacity. The training in Cape Town seemed to offer the best available, hence my choice. To reach there involved a long train journey. We were living near Salisbury, Southern Rhodesia, at the time, and twenty miles south was Norton Station on the railway line down to Bulawayo. Having scrambled up into the overnight train at that platformless isolated rural stop, I can still remember sharing a small compartment with five strangers. Climbing up into the top bunk of narrow, hard green leather, the night was spent lying awake feeling numb, but also wondering what lay ahead. The old steam engine just steadily chugged southwards and early the next morning arrived safely in Bulawayo. It seemed very lonely as I transferred to the waiting train headed for Cape Town, which would take me a further two nights and days away from the last home I had known.

In the new compartment were five others making the journey southwards and one of those was a lovely girl who would be starting nursing with me at Groote Schuur Hospital. Rose was friendly and invited me to go with her to the carriage holding several medical students returning to Cape Town university after their vacation, one of whom was Rose's brother, Stuart. They were all Christians and for the rest of the journey the group of us spent much time together singing songs, choruses, hymns, and just thoroughly enjoying the hours. How different from my expectations!

Rose became a very dear friend, and we still enjoy that rich friendship some five decades later, despite the miles between. But in those days I believe they were God's love for me in human form. Stuart knew his way around that area of the Cape after several years of study at Cape Town university and was already settled in a local church, so he just introduced Rose and me to them. The years at Stellenberg Chapel in Pinelands, Cape Town were to provide a deep foundation of caring, teaching and a thorough grounding in God's Word, which stood me in good stead for all the years ahead. They became my church family, with a lively young people's work.

Having spent the morning gazing out of the train window at the amazing mountain scenery of the Hex River Mountain Pass we gradually descended several thousand feet from the high plateaus of the interior (height 3,000-5,000ft) to sea level. Arriving in Cape Town my new friends were again the ones who knew the way and led me forward. Rose and I had enrolled in the three and a half years' training to be Registered Nurses and were issued with starchy white uniforms and caps. What a sight we looked!

Obviously new! Five of about forty of us who began PTS training.

Thus began the first two months of Preliminary Training School (PTS), where we were taught all the basics needed for a new nurse to go on to the wards – how to make beds, ensure a patient's comfort, do bed baths, give bedpans, clean the sluice room and innumerable other basic practical issues. From there we moved on to start our years in Groote Schuur Hospital.

New friendships were formed. A lovely friend from that time was perhaps the shortest girl in the group. She was amazing. One parent was Afrikaans, the other German, and she grew up to use both those languages and English fluently. In fact, in one short conversation together in her home, she would easily change from one language to the other, depending on whom she was addressing at the time. She never seemed to mix them up.

Friendship with Rose grew too and we were soon joined by another Christian, Bonny. The three of us went through our years of training together. Bonny married and she and her husband became missionaries in Papua New Guinea. Many years later Bonny died of cancer resulting from a chronic bowel condition from which she suffered through all the years we knew her.

The long and the short of it!
Cape Town 1958.

It was good to be part of such a group of friends, and another new experience for me.

Nursing training days

Groote Schuur Hospital, situated on the slopes of Table Mountain, had 1,000 beds and was, at that time, the largest hospital under one roof in the southern hemisphere. It was run very differently from a hospital today. Most of the wards were the old 'Nightingale' style with a twenty-bed section for women, another for men and a few side rooms. Our sisters were martinets who expected and got obedience. In addition to our board, we earned the princely sum of thirty shillings a month, for which we were officially working sixty hours a week (plus unpaid overtime), spent three months of every year on night duty ... and loved it! In the winter the night matron demanded that we open all the windows and the patio doors at the end of the ward, even when the snow lay on Table Mountain and wind blew off it right down the slopes and straight into the ward! *'Nurse, you can give the patients extra blankets if they are cold. The fresh air is good for them!'* We poor nurses were not allowed to roll down our sleeves or wear our cloaks in the wards, so had to keep moving!

During our training days we worked in rotation through all the wards and in theatre, both on day and night duty. Night duty meant twelve hours a night for twelve nights before having two nights off, and was repeated annually for three months at a stretch. If we were scheduled right, we occasionally had four nights off in a row – what a treat! But, like most things, we grew used to night duty as well as all the other challenges that the training brought. Dr Christiaan Barnard was doing major and experimental heart surgery at the time. I well remember one night-duty rota in theatre when we had to set up all the huge machines used for heart bypass surgery. The room seemed to be wall-to-wall machinery. It was a few years after we left that Barnard successfully transplanted the first adult heart.

Life during those years was full. We worked long hours, but played well too. There was a really large, keen young people's group (nursing and varsity ages) in our church and we had good relationships. In addition there were many other Christian young people in the area. Many were the evenings we spent out on the slopes of Table Mountain, or down at the beach, having a *braai* (barbecue). One of our group was a gifted musician and he always had his accordion to hand, leading us in singing, praise and worship together. It seemed in those days we were singing whenever we met together. An added bonus for us nurses was that there was usually someone with a car willing to collect us when we finished work at unusual hours, thus enabling us to be part of the different activities.

Susie

Susie was a young lady, probably in her late teens at the time, who had a tumour high up on her spine. When the surgeons removed the tumour they were convinced that her spinal nerves were destroyed and that she would never stand or walk again; in fact, they were amazed that she had even lived through the surgery. From my memory of the time, they stated to the staff that she would be completely paralysed from the neck downwards even if she did survive. I was still a young student nurse, working on the neurological ward under a dedicated sister, who was a Christian. She and another Afrikaans nurse shared with me the story that unfolded over many weeks.

Susie was indeed paralysed after surgery and we nursed her on what was known as a Stryker bed,[6] so that she could easily be turned regularly without danger of further damaging her spine. There was no Intensive Therapy Unit (ITU) in those days and her care was intensive and demanding as she was only one of the patients on that busy ward. My first clear memory of Susie herself was that whenever we had turned her to lie facing downwards, looking towards the old hospital floor (some 18in below) through the opening created to allow her to breathe, she would ask me to open and arrange her Bible on the floor so she could read it to herself. She was

---

[6] The Stryker bed was a special frame which allowed handling of patients in a way that protected their serious back injuries.

unable to move her arms or legs, so I had to go back often and turn the pages for her.

Susie loved the Lord Jesus and found strength and hope in His Word. She spoke Afrikaans and had an Afrikaans Bible. I struggled with my schoolgirl knowledge of that language, but we became fellow Christians walking her difficult road together.

Then came even worse days. Susie's legs began to curl up in very painful spasms, uncontrollable and devastating to her. Up to that point she had held on to her belief that she would be healed, but the pain was just too much. Gradually the spine and surgical wound healed and the consultants decided that she could be moved onto a normal-style bed, but must remain absolutely flat or she would probably faint, or possibly her heart would stop. Very gradually the sister and I, after the doctors' rounds, began to raise her head in the adjustable bed and over a period of many days had her sitting up. By that time she had begun to have some movement in her arms and, with support, could turn the pages of her Bible again. The day came when we raised the head of her bed before the doctors arrived. They were flabbergasted at her progress.

Susie herself was the pleading instigator of each step we took. The next hurdle came when she wanted to sit in a chair and the doctors were again very sceptical. We used to lift her out of bed after the doctors' rounds, for longer and longer periods each day. She still had a catheter in place so managed very well. Then came the day when she pleaded to have the catheter removed so she could learn control herself. By that time the stunned doctors were more easily persuaded, although still believed that there was no way she would recover bladder and bowel control. Sister, who by now was convinced that Susie would recover fully despite the doctors' pessimism, produced a bedpan, the likes of which I have never seen before or since. It was inflatable, so soft, and we placed it on the chair, then Susie sat on that as her cushion. Except for unwanted reverberations at times, it did what was needed!

Then came the day when she wanted to begin to stand and walk. (I am not sure why, but I do not remember any physiotherapists being there to help us in those days.) So again after having been seen by the doctors, we helped Susie to begin to bear weight on her legs, then gradually to gain strength and movement. Soon afterwards she was discharged from hospital in a wheelchair, so we no longer were able to monitor her progress. As a gift for that Christmas of 1959 she gave me a copy of Mrs Chas E Cowman's daily readings, *Streams in the Desert*.[7] I have the book in front of me at the moment, with a message in it: 'To dear Michie, with much love and thankfulness, from Susie.' (Of course in those days we did not use Christian names at work.) She herself had an Afrikaans version of the book, which she had used while in hospital and knew I appreciated it.

That would have been the end of this story, except that many months later I was sent down to the outpatients' department situated in the basement under the hospital. Suddenly someone came running clumsily up the sloping

---

[7] Mrs Chas E Cowman, *Streams in the Desert*, fifteenth edition 1935 (original published Los Angeles, CA: Oriental Mission Society, 1925).

corridor calling my name and threw herself into my arms. It was Susie! She was not just able to walk but even, to some degree, run. She would always be clumsy and rather uncoordinated, but was fully mobile without even her wheelchair. Never having really seen her mobile and standing alone, one of the biggest surprises for me was how short she was. What a joy to see such wonderful answers to our prayers.

Towards the end of my second year of nursing I had run down the six flights of stairs from the ward to the pharmacy. It was nearing closing time and we urgently needed some medication or other. Reaching almost the last section of the stairs, I turned for the next flight and my rubber-soled shoe stuck firmly on the rubber-edged tread of the stair. It did not turn with me. Result: one ankle injury. It hurt a bit at the time, but I went on to the pharmacy. On the way back to the ward, I took the lift!

Having bound it up with a crepe bandage, I finished the shift and hobbled off home to our flat at the bottom of the hill below the hospital, shared with two other Christian friends. The ankle hurt, but I was off for the weekend so there would be time to recover. Our church youth leader happened to drop in on his way home from work and when he saw me, sent my friend to pack a bag and took me to their home. There he, his wife and their three delightful small sons cared for me all weekend.

By Monday it was obvious that the ankle would not allow me to return to work, so I reported to the nurses' sickbay, then was sent on to orthopaedic outpatients. Well I remember being a guinea pig for the student doctors!

The consultant had diagnosed a rarely seen injury to the stabilising ligaments encircling the ankle and he proceeded, with my permission, to demonstrate it to the medical students. He would rotate my foot and every time it hurt and I squirmed, he said, 'You see.' The treatment was either immediate surgery or six weeks in a plaster-of-Paris cast, which apparently usually did not work. He was reluctant to do the surgery without first trying to see if it would heal itself while in the cast, and so began a break from my training. Travelling back to Salisbury, it was a pleasant time with my family and I returned to Cape Town fully expecting the ankle to be healed. Despite my prayers, it wasn't! After further X-rays and examination I was booked for an urgent major repair operation the following Monday.

Sunday evening found me kneeling by my bed and praying. I probably talked with the Lord about the surgery the next day. But, unasked for, it was as though a voice said to me, 'Your ankle is healed and you should go back to work tomorrow.' It came totally out of the blue and I was filled with amazement. Although accepting it was God speaking, I really wondered what was going to happen the next morning. After a sound night's sleep I woke, dressed in my uniform and went to the hospital early. Entering through the outpatients' department, to my amazement I met the consultant's registrar. He was a Christian and so, when I told him my story, was more prepared to accept it than most. In my wariness I asked for the surgery to be put off for a week or two to make sure it was healed, but he went on to challenge me by saying that the consultant orthopaedic surgeon was going off on six weeks' leave on Wednesday and if he did not operate today could not do so for at least six weeks. That surgeon was the only one experienced enough to operate on a person with such an injury. Swallowing hard, I accepted that delay and prepared to return to work, but then had to face matron. That would not be so easy!

Having gone up to matron's office, only her deputy was available, who was much more approachable. Telling her my tale, I asked to be allocated to a ward. Her response challenged me anew. She said that the only place she had a need for a nurse at the moment was on ward A5, always known as the busiest ward in the hospital. Swallowing hard again, I accepted the placement. Despite an aching ankle, I worked for the next six weeks on A5, doing our usual quota of sixty hours a week, plus overtime every day except one. Gradually the ache eased and my ankle was fully healed. Later the consultant was to examine it, check his notes and the X-rays and discharge me from his care, finding it hard to believe but convinced that it was healed and stable. Sometimes we have to take God at His word even when all the absolute proof is not there, and the challenge of that day has often reminded me that we have to trust Him even when, as then, the ankle still ached.

In Pinelands in those days were a young couple, Eric and Nancy. At the time they had three young sons under seven. Eric was an elder and the youth leader at Stellenberg Chapel, where we worshipped. They ran the Friday night 'squash' for the young people (mainly eighteen- to twenty-five-year-olds) and we were indeed packed tightly into their living room each week. Eric and Nancy opened their home to many, but for me it became a very special place and I had a key to the door with a welcome at any time. They became dear friends, and through their love and support I began to really grow in understanding what the Christian life was all about. God's Word challenged me and I was baptised by immersion as a personal testimony of my commitment to Christ. Later they were also a real support through all my years at Lukolwe.

Eric was an evangelist at heart and through the years God used him to lead many people to a personal relationship with Jesus. He had a particular influence on my family. Through his ministry, when they were visiting Cape Town, my father and brother eventually came to accept Christ as Saviour and my mother's lapsed relationship with the Lord was renewed. The difference it made to our home in Salisbury was that on my next trip back on holiday we sat together as a family around an open fire. The fireplace had been built (in that house that was being slowly constructed as they could afford it), and replaced the cocktail cabinet which had previously hidden the gaping hole below the chimney.

Perhaps this is a good time to tell you a little about them.

A tale of three people

The first was a boy born in Scotland in 1911, the son of a blacksmith. In the early 1920s his parents left post-war

Scotland and emigrated to Detroit, USA. There, in his teenage years, he became the leader of the young people in a large Baptist church youth group. He was involved in all their activities and enjoyed the fellowship with the other young people, but never actually knew for himself the personal relationship with Jesus that was at the centre of the church's teaching.

The second, a girl, was born in the same year, also in Scotland and not too far from where the boy had lived. Her family also emigrated to the United States when she was in her teens. She joined the same youth group, yet there was a profound, but subtle, difference. The girl had a personal relationship with Jesus that had changed her life, and was baptised during those years. The boy was just part of the crowd.

In the process of time he followed her family back across the Atlantic to England, and later they married. Sunday was the only day they could spend together, so they usually went out on his motorbike. The husband worked long hours including overtime every Saturday for a full year in order to buy his wife a piano. That only made their Sundays a more precious time to spend together. Gradually all church attendance dropped away.

For the man, who had just enjoyed the outward pleasure of being part of a group of young people, that was no problem, but ... for the woman there were many periods of distress and feeling guilty. Gradually she stopped reading her Bible each day, stopped talking with Jesus, and she slowly lost the desire to worship Him.

To their grief no child was born despite nearly five years with no menstrual periods and many treatments.

Then they were accepted for adoption. Shortly after the outbreak of the Second World War, to their and the doctor's amazement, she fell pregnant with a baby girl. Later they also had a baby boy.

A further twenty-odd years followed during which she sent her two children to Sunday school and occasionally took them to a church service. But she never showed by life or action the commitment she had made to Jesus Christ. The wonderful thing is that the God who had placed His life within her never let her go.

One day when her daughter, who was training as a nurse, was on holiday at home and asked her mother's permission to take an old Scofield Bible[8] back to Cape Town. It was sitting in the bookcase in the daughter's room and had clearly lain unopened for a very long time. That Bible had been much loved and well marked, and was quite dog-eared. The mother looked sadly at her old Bible and grieved, but could find no reason to refuse the request. After all, she *never* used it herself!

I said that it was a tale of three people. As you may have guessed, I was that daughter, the baby born when they had given up hope. I had come into a personal relationship with Jesus Christ, to love Him and to love His Word. Reading my mother's old well-marked Bible was the first time I began to wonder about her faith.

Some time later they travelled down to visit me in Cape Town. During that holiday they were drawn into a loving caring church, where people really showed them

---

[8] The Scofield Reference Bible, Authorised Version (Oxford: Oxford University Press, 1917).

God's love. For Mum it woke the small germ of true life within her and she asked God's forgiveness for the many years during which she had turned her back on Him. Her whole heart cried out to God for a renewed relationship and she wept over the wasted years between. One of the special things of that time was that I was able to hand Mum back her very own well-loved Bible that had been so special to her. God was so good.

My father was challenged by the message of God's love for him, but refused to submit to the authority and love of God. His pride gave battle! It took several months more of struggle before he finally knelt down and asked God to forgive his sins, to cleanse and heal him, and to take control of his life.

My story, the third person of our tale, was different too. My father had had all the outward trappings of Christianity as he led the young people there in Detroit. But he had not had real life – that inner relationship with God. It took another thirty hard years before he finally allowed God to work the miracle in him of changing his life from the inside out. My mother, on the other hand, had truly committed her life to Jesus as Lord. She had been baptised by immersion as a teenager, on the confession of her faith. Although she had turned her back on God through the intervening years, His life was still within her.

> For God so loved the world that he gave his one
> and only Son, that whoever believes in him shall
> not perish but have eternal life.
> (John 3:16)

My story followed a different pattern. Although Jesus was not mentioned in our home as I grew up, I came to a personal acceptance of Jesus Christ and His death for me on the cross. He gave me life. He is the King of kings, so I am the daughter of the King, but also a servant of the same King, and it is a joy to serve Him. He has directed and controlled my life in many ways. He led me through nursing and midwifery training, a short time at Bible school and then many years as a missionary nurse in Zambia.

For all three of us, God created us in love. He gave us the ability to choose. That choice relates to our relationship with Him as well as other aspects of our lives. What we choose about Him will affect every corner of our lives.

> Now fear the LORD and serve him with all faithfulness ... But if serving the LORD seems undesirable to you, *then choose for yourselves this day whom you will serve* ... But as for me and my household, we will serve the LORD.
> (Joshua 24:14-15, my emphasis)

For my father the outward trappings of Christianity were useful while he could be involved as a leader of the young people. But when it interfered with what he wanted to do in life, it was not important. His choices could be described as selfish and for his own pleasure.

My mum had indeed surrendered to the lordship of Jesus Christ, and chosen to go His way. She allowed love for Dad and other things to come between herself and the

God she loved and whose Spirit lived within her. It took many hard, barren, wasted years before that flicker of life was rekindled and she chose to walk God's way.

For me, my walk was different too. It was one of fairly steady growth in the knowledge and love of God. He led me into a life that was not particularly easy, but full of joy as I serve Him. There have been up and downs in the conscious relationship with Him through the years, but He is always trustworthy.

Midwifery

I had started nursing believing that that was what God wanted of me, with a view to serving Him in some mission capacity, and that midwifery would be an essential part of that. After our general training, which had taken more than three and a half years, Rose and I wanted to go to the UK for our midwifery training. From the obscurity of southern Africa, Guy's Hospital ('Guy's') in London sounded an attractive name to us, so we applied and were accepted for the first half of our training. Looking back I have to laugh at how we had made our plans for training at a 'big name' hospital and yet God overruled to give me the best obstetric preparation I could get for the years ahead – but I did not know it then.

Following the initial interview at Guy's in April 1963 we had just two weeks before starting the course, but very little money with which to plan a holiday. Rose's aunt encouraged us to hitchhike, and we did so travelling from London up to Scotland, all around Scotland and back to London. With many adventures, lots of laughter and miles of walking, we had a wonderful time. Even the weather did not deter us. We had crossed the equator in the baking heat one Friday, had the interview at Guy's, and a week later we were in a snow storm in Glasgow! We bought warm jackets, gloves and waterproof plastic raincoats which protected us from the cold and the many days of rain. Staying in youth hostels was a new experience, sometimes very good, but at others, challenging. One evening on the banks of Loch Ness we were so cold that we collected large smooth round boulders and put them in the oven. They warmed our beds effectively that night, although I later learned that it was rather a dangerous idea as the water content could have caused them to explode with the heat, having come from the water's edge at the side of the loch.

Travelling from Oban to Fort William there was dull steady rain and very low cloud as we walked out of the town, across the Connel Bridge, and onto the road to Fort William. We looked bedraggled, dressed in white plastic raincoats over thick jackets and with packs on our backs. The passing cars did not seem inclined to pick up the hitchhikers. One couldn't blame them!

After several miles, a car passed us at full speed, but then stopped a distance down the road. When we reached it the driver had the boot open, and very brusquely told us to take off our backpacks, then our coats and jackets, and put them in the boot. He seemed far from friendly, and if his wife had not been in the car we would have refused the lift, although by that time the weather had almost beaten us. It was so cold and wet.

At first it was uncomfortable in the car. The wife tried to make conversation, but the silent driver was rather dour. Soon, in reply to her queries, interest grew in learning we were from Rhodesia and why we were hitchhiking around Scotland, the birth land of both sets of our parents. Gradually her husband joined in the general conversation. Apparently he had been convinced that we might be carrying guns and stated that his wife had made him stop. The outcome was a glorious day. The sun came out and the views were magnificent. The couple had planned to use the Ballachulish Ferry at the narrows of Loch Leven, but then decided to take the long road route around the sea loch just to show us the beauty of it. At the furthest end of the loch we stopped and all enjoyed a delicious picnic tea, produced from the boot of the car. After they had taken us right to the door of the youth hostel, we parted the best of acquaintances.

On the return journey from Edinburgh in the cab of a lorry we were stopped by the police, who were looking for two girls who had broken out from a reformatory. That was scary as they were abrupt, refused to let our driver assist us and would not tell us why they had targeted us. By that stage in our journey we probably looked scruffy enough to raise their awareness! After scrambling over the load in the back of the lorry to retrieve our passports from our backpacks, they were finally satisfied and we continued on our way.

That holiday was one of those spur-of-the-moment decisions resulting in an amazing time we would probably never have experienced if we had stopped long enough to think too hard about it.

The midwifery course was divided into two separate parts of six months. The first part of our training at Guy's turned out to be three months each at Guy's and Hackney hospitals. At Guy's they trained us well in the theory and in the care before and after the birth of a baby, but there were too many medical students for us to see much of babies actually being born. Yet it was a good solid foundation for what was to come!

The second three months of the course was at Hackney Hospital in the East End of London. That was an education in itself. It was from the sublime to the ridiculous! There we experienced many babies born, but, more importantly, many deliveries with similar complications to those I would later to see in the bush in Zambia. Diseases that are unique to the Afro-Caribbean races were common there, such as sickle-cell anaemia with its potentially devastating effect. Years later memories of experiences at Hackney came back when needed, enabling me to know how to respond or where to look up textbooks for help in crisis situations. Much of what we learned was typified by the first TV series *Call the Midwife*,[9] set only a few years earlier in that same area of London. How medicine has changed.

For the second part of our training as pupil midwives we chose to apply to a course in Exeter. Again, God allowed it to be so much better that we could have imagined. The experience there prepared me in unexpected ways for the unknown future. Half of those six months was spent in a hospital focusing on women

---

[9] A series of programmes run over several years on BBC 1.

who had potentially complicated pregnancies and labour, and the final three months working on the district in people's own homes. We did enjoy those months of hard work, laughter and fun. Working as a district midwife had surprising similarities to what I was later to experience in the rural isolation of work in Zambia.

After qualifying I then worked for a few months as a district midwife before going to Capernwray Winter Bible School which was very influential in my understanding and love of God's Word. That six months of concentrated study was centred on the Scriptures and very valuable.

It was a full two years before I returned to Rhodesia in April 1965.

Giving ... and receiving

When I first came to England for midwifery training, I began putting £5 a month into a Post Office savings account. It was towards my going to a Bible school or, if not me, to enable someone else to go. At the time our student salary was very small. When the time came to apply for Capernwray Bible School, the cost of the six months, including board, was around £83. That was a lot of money in those days (now the cost is more than £6,000). But by then the special account held a total of £85, so covered it adequately. What a lesson that was to me in trusting God for His supply. At the start of the fund I had no knowledge of how long it would be maintained, or even of a place of study like Capernwray.

For that Christmas holiday season, while at Capernwray, I knew that I had a temporary job as a district midwife waiting for me back in Exeter and enough money to travel there by coach. But that was 1964/65 winter and very heavy snow came down early in December. A gift of money unexpectedly arrived in the mail and enabled me to change my plans from the coach trip to travelling by train. The trains managed to get through, although many hours late, but the coaches were completely snowed in. Without that special gift it would not have been possible to reach Exeter for the work to which I had made a commitment. The person who sent the money was used as God's provision for a need I had not even anticipated. God provides in many ways.

After the years in England, I returned to my parents' home in Salisbury, Rhodesia. One Sunday morning I was reading God's Word and talking with Him and felt very clearly that God was saying I should give my last £5 (probably equivalent in purchasing power to at least £500 now) to a special friend, Alison, whom I was to see later that day. I argued with God, as my friend was earning a good salary, whereas I had literally no income and no job and only that £5 left. But I decided to put the money in an envelope with a note to say why I was giving it and slipped it into her handbag as she drove us out to have dinner with other friends.

Later that evening it was a very tearful Alison who phoned me after reaching home. She had opened the envelope and, as a result, was able to buy her mother's essential blood pressure medication the next morning. By my obedience God had provided for her very real need.

But God is no person's debtor and as we were leaving our mutual friend's home after the Sunday meal, her husband came up to the car and passed me an envelope through the window. In it there was a £10 note! Later on I grew more accustomed to God's amazing provision for me, but that day I learned a lesson in obedience from a great and loving Father, one that I have never forgotten –

in fact more than fifty years later I still thrill at the memory.

Someone has said that God does not waste any experiences and many is the time when that has been true in daily living. During my nursing and midwifery training days, skills were learned that were to be invaluable later when caring for a maternity patient in labour or a desperately ill person in hospital. Sometimes when there were life-threatening problems the care given was based on memories, built on skills learned, with a textbook on the bed before me and arrow prayers flowing to a heavenly Father.

Then, later in life, after leaving Lukolwe, some of the life experiences learned during those years in the bush in Zambia translated into wisdom for others here today. It was all part of the patchwork kaleidoscope of preparation for what lay ahead. And so it goes on.

But more of that later.

What next?

Very early in my first period of nursing training in Cape Town I heard a missionary lady from Northern Rhodesia (later Zambia) sharing how desperately they needed a nurse for a new work that had started the previous year in an isolated north-west area. Although there was no trained medical person among the mission staff, the local people had started coming for medical help and for the birth of their babies. This laid a burden on my heart to pray for that nurse. It was obvious to me, at that time, that I could not be that person. There was still at least five years' training ahead before I would be available to go anywhere – I was sure that midwifery training was essential and considered some Bible school training too. But I prayed and continued to pray, fully expecting God to answer promptly when the need seemed so urgent.

Five years later, after returning to Rhodesia from the UK, it was clear to me (and to others) that God was leading me to that isolated place in north-west Zambia, a centre of Bible teaching, outreach and the beginnings of medical work, called Lukolwe. The nearest town was 550 miles away, taking at least two days' journey over rough dirt roads.

Having been interested in the medical work at Lukolwe and also having expected someone else to be the answer to my prayers for a nurse, I gradually began to wonder if I was supposed to be that person. Then began the inner battle, questioning whether this was my will or God's plan. Cape Town was the hub of most mission work in southern Africa, as in those days overseas travel was mainly by sea, so during our years there we were inevitably kept in touch with many missionaries. During the two years in England, there had been far less contact with or news from Zambia and I had a growing number of questions regarding the next step in my life. A lovely couple in Exeter, both doctors and he an elder in the local church I attended, encouraged me to make contact with Echoes of Service (now Echoes International) who support mission work and churches all over the world. One day a friend and I drove from Exeter to Bath for an arranged interview with the staff there, beginning what was to become many years of a fruitful working relationship.

It was amazing that we even reached Bath that day. The early morning drive through the beauty of the winding country roads from Exeter to Bath was special. (There were no motorways.) We enjoyed our friendship and chatted happily. Some time into the journey my friend overtook a slow lorry, pulled in safely and we continued on our way. At the time of overtaking the driver of an oncoming car had hooted violently at us, but beyond a laugh together we had just ignored it. Gill's driving was good and we had overtaken very safely. Some considerable time later a speeding car overtook us, then cut in front of us, forcing us to stop on the empty narrow country road. Then the driver proceeded to yell and shout at us both. His language was extreme and we were both very shocked. It was our first exposure to what was later called 'road rage'. Thankfully, beyond the shouting and a few thumps on the roof of our car, there were no physical injuries. He just walked away, climbed into his car, turned around and drove back the way he had come. We felt we needed some resuscitation!

The inner battle as to whether going to Lukolwe was just a selfish desire or really God's plan for me continued through the six months at Capernwray Bible School. That year there were 120 of us students, from twenty-one different countries, and the intense teaching of the Bible as a whole was both challenging and powerful in my life. Because the atmosphere at Capernwray was centred on God's Word and service, I was able to focus on the 'What next' question. I was still praying for the nurse to go to Lukolwe, but increasingly wondering if I was the one who should answer that prayer. Financially I had no savings, having already paid my return fares from and back to Africa and then the costs of Bible school with the little I had earned. What lay ahead?

One day I talked this over with a godly elderly man, Arnold Pickering, who had come to lecture us for the week. We had first met on that visit to Echoes in Bath. Sharing with him my uncertainty, he pointed to the verse in Isaiah where it says: 'Every valley shall be exalted, and every mountain and hill shall be made low: and the crooked shall be made straight, and the rough places plain' (Isaiah 40:4, KJV). He reminded me that valleys can feel like very dark places and mountains impossible climbs, but life does take us up and over and down again into the valleys, then the long climb up again. Sometimes we have to slog through the valleys and force ourselves to climb the mountains until the day when we are fit and strong again – then we have a new joy and the valleys do not seem so low, or the mountains so unscalable.

Do you mark your Bible and sometimes put the date beside a verse? I do so from time to time when it has been something very special. Perhaps that was the first time.

Yet a loving heavenly Father knew I still did not trust myself and sent another challenge, the outcome of which was to leave me eventually with a certainty of His leading when I finally went to Lukolwe. While I was at Capernwray, a senior missionary couple approached me, asking me to consider going to a mission medical centre in Zaire (now Democratic Republic of Congo), to relieve two overworked missionary nurses for a year, before going to Lukolwe.

This came close to the time I was about to return to my parents' home in Salisbury, Rhodesia, after two years in England. The couple continued their gentle pressure during the two weeks as we travelled together by ship back to Cape Town. In my naivety I was persuaded to consider this option, particularly as, in theory, the initial visit would be a short free trip travelling with them.

Another issue was the dangerous state of life in Zaire at that time of uprising and conflict. I knew that my going there would be an even harder decision for my parents to accept. Finally, after some consideration and prayer, I agreed to go on the visit, but only if I was able to pay a visit to Lukolwe in Zambia on the same trip. That seemed a very feasible option to me as I looked at a map, and it would allow me to experience both places. But that did not sit comfortably with their plans to draw me permanently to Zaire in order to fill what they saw as an urgent need. Unhappy about this condition, they still appeared to agree with the request. I was ignorant of the difficulties of travel in that part of the world, but they knew that practically it would prove very difficult, if not impossible, to arrange the trip to Lukolwe as well. Applications began for a visa for me to visit Zaire.

The next evening I attended a missionary meeting where a young man was sharing about his recent experience of visiting Malawi. During the visit he felt clarity in the knowledge that it was where God wanted him and his family to work. From a human point of view it should have reinforced my plan to pay a visit to Zaire, but it had the opposite effect. All my doubts rose anew.

Going to my room that night I knelt by my bed and struggled with the Lord over it all. Oh, how I argued, shared my doubts and just cried out to Him. After all, it was only a visit … wouldn't cost anything extra … they had started to apply for the visa … and so on. Finally, I said to the Lord that if I was not to go, I was prepared to cancel all plans for the trip and wait for God's leading onwards. I climbed into bed well after midnight and, with a deep peace in my heart, turned over and slept soundly. At 5am I woke absolutely sure that I was to cancel all the plans and then phoned Crawford Allison, an older wise missionary friend whom I knew would be up doing Bible translation work from 4.30 every morning. I simply told him about the doubts and my decision and his immediate comment was: 'When in doubt, don't.' He was very supportive and disregarded the work he had already done on my behalf for the visa application.

Then I had to tell the couple of my changed decision. They were considerably less gracious. They asked to meet with me for lunch and to discuss it. My mother accompanied me, an unusual thing in itself. They tried every argument they could think of to make me change my mind and it was an unpleasant time, but deep within was that peace that had flooded my soul the night before. That difficult conversation helped me to begin to fully realise some of their motivation and pressure regarding the trip, but I remained firm in my decision. If it had not been for Crawford's encouragement earlier that day it might even have been a different outcome, but that deep peace within enabled me to take the stand I needed. It was only later, when we arrived home and I heard my mother telling Dad of her anger at the pressure they had tried to exert to make me go on the visit that I began realistically to see it for what it was.

Can you envisage how I felt by then? Emotionally battered and bruised in so many ways and uncertain of what came next. I had already 'blown it' once and now what should I do? Was my interest in Lukolwe valid? I had made one mistake and was afraid of making another, so hesitated to make any decisions. At that time Dad did something he had never done before – nor ever did again. He quietly said to me that the money was in the bank for me to fly up on a visit to Lukolwe. No pressure, but it was there when I needed it.

The next week we were having an evening meal with friends and our host's father was on his way from Lukolwe to the UK. Elderly Mr Sims had worked in that area for very many years and had been part of the start of the actual residential work at Lukolwe seven years earlier. Although we did not know it then, he already had cancer and only lived another year. During the evening together he called me aside privately and gave me a ten-shilling Zambian note he had 'left over', saying quietly, 'This is for when you visit Lukolwe, in case you need some local cash.' A statement of fact that I later learned stemmed from a deep belief that I was the one who would be going there long-term. But he put no other pressure on me by word or action.

With the above two sources of encouragement and after making contact with the family at Lukolwe, I booked the flights up to the local township of Balovale (later called Zambezi), some sixty miles from Lukolwe.

That trip was an education in itself. Flying out from Salisbury very early in the morning, on a largish commercial plane, we landed in Lusaka, Zambia. (Northern Rhodesia had changed to Zambia at independence in 1964, the previous year.) The airport consisted of two old tin Nissan huts (ex-wartime) and not much more. In preparation for the next section of the journey we, the passengers, were taken to huge scales and weighed together with our luggage! The plane was a six-seater Beaver. Known as the 'Land Rover of the air', it was small and sturdy and very good for that type of bush flight. To my eyes it just looked crude and clumsy!

The first section was a two-hour flight due west and fairly high to Mongu, where most of the passengers left us and several others joined for the short ten-minute hop over the Zambezi River to Kalabo – a dry arid landing strip and not much else. Onwards from there I was the only passenger, so sat next to the pilot and, in deference to my intense air sickness, we flew low for the rest of the way, following the Zambezi River. Often we were below tree level looking out at the many hippos and crocodiles. Flying over Chitokoloki (pronounced *Chi-toe-koe-loe-ki*) Mission we were so low that it was fun to watch the missionaries' faces as they came out of buildings to look up at the low-flying aircraft and wave to us.

After travelling all day, when finally landing in Balovale in the late afternoon I was relieved to know that that part of the journey was over. Being invited and having sent messages well ahead, I had fully expected to be met when we arrived at Balovale airport. The plane took off on its return flight and I was left alone on the dirt airstrip with my case beside me, unsure of the next step. No one appeared. It was barren and dry, with no staff or other evidence of activity.

Some time later a Land Rover came rolling in and a cheerful voice asked whether I was waiting for someone. Chuckling cheerfully, and proclaiming that it was not unusual for there to be no one around, the man introduced me to his wife. Thus I met Bill and Vi Collias, who were to become special friends. Bill had a transportation and building business and they had both been born and lived in the area all their lives. They loaded up the 'stray' and took me off to their home for a meal and to await news as to whether or not someone was coming to collect me.

Some hours later, after dark, a muddy pickup drove into the yard. My transport had arrived! That was my first taste of the difficulty with communication that was so common through all the years I was there. The folk at Lukolwe (pronounced *Loo-ko-lway*) had only heard on the two-way radio at five-thirty that afternoon of my possible arrival (ie when I had actually already landed in Balovale) and proceeded to ask the missionaries at Chavuma to try to collect me. Ben had come down to Balovale and we drove back the further fifty miles (two hours) to Chavuma over a very rough dirt road. Ben explained to me that I would be staying in their home at Chavuma Mission tonight as it was not possible to cross the Zambezi River in the dark.

As time passed I too learned to live with those communication limitations and the unexpected complications that occasionally developed, but that night felt exhausted and scarcely coping by the time we arrived at Chavuma. I had been travelling since early morning, intensely airsick and among strangers in a very different environment. There all the missionaries had gathered together to share a meal and welcome me. On arrival I was escorted to my room and left to 'freshen up'. The trouble was that there were no ceilings in the house, not even in the bathroom, and everyone could hear every movement I made. So, to give me privacy, they all started to sing together – and sounded like a huge choir.

Weary from a long and exciting day and feeling shy and embarrassed, I ventured out to meet so many new faces with no hope of remembering the names of folk who were soon to become good friends. There were only fifteen of them. It felt like an army! What a group of genuinely friendly people, but that night their caring nearly undid this exhausted traveller. Sleep proved restless, under a mosquito net for the first time, but with geckos (little lizards) and other insects crawling over the outside and mosquitoes buzzing around.

Next day we braved the Zambezi River by means of a dugout canoe, made from one single tree trunk. It did not feel very stable. I was met on the other bank by some of the Lukolwe family and driven the ten miles (one hour) back to Lukolwe. It was amazing to arrive and be so genuinely welcomed – this guest who had appeared out of the blue to stay for six weeks.

Over the next few days, as I read my daily Bible readings, learned more of the life there and so on, it became clearer and clearer both to me and the other missionaries that this was where God wanted me to work. It was challenging and would not be easy. Days were full of new things, yet from the beginning I felt so at home. Within a short time I was convinced this was where God was leading me long-term, but I did have one worry.

The thing that bothered me most was the knowledge that we were in the tropics and the hot season (September to November), when it was building up to the rains, would be very hot indeed. Even during schooldays in Salisbury, far south, I had not coped well with the hot season and suffered from severe migraines. At Lukolwe it would be hotter. How was I going to cope? Really anxious, I talked with the Lord about it one night and specifically asked Him for wisdom. Waking the next morning for my usual quiet time, the passage for the day was from Jeremiah. It contained the words, which, in the NIV 2011 translation read:

> But blessed is the one who trusts in the Lord, whose confidence is in him.
> They will be like a tree planted by the water that sends out its roots by the stream.
> It does not fear when heat comes; its leaves are always green.
> It has no worries in a year of drought and never fails to bear fruit.
> (Jeremiah 17:7-8)

How could I fear? He was giving me the promise of fruitfulness even during the heat. To me, that morning, it was as if God was saying I need not be anxious as He was in control. The promise of those verses remained true all the years I was at Lukolwe. I did not like the heat, but never had to give up because of it.

Interestingly, in those days I think I equated fruitfulness with activity, but later came to realise that it was rather walking, and continuing to live in obedience to the Holy Spirit's direction. Like trees planted by the water we need to bear the fruit God plans for us individually.

After six weeks, and in agreement with the other missionaries there, I went home to Salisbury and applied for a visa for long-term residence in Zambia. Packing my few possessions, I booked the bus journey back to the Copperbelt, as I couldn't afford another plane flight. The relevant visa arrived in the mail a mere twenty-four hours before I was to board the bus. It was for an indefinite stay, and all I needed. It was only later that I learned that, within the following few weeks, other missionaries arriving to work in different, but similar, locations nearer the town received visas for only two years at a time. That would have made my life very difficult indeed, because Lukolwe was so isolated.

Six weeks after leaving the country I was on my way back by bus to the Zambian Copperbelt, a central area of several towns including Chingola, Kitwe, Luanshya and Ndola, based around the copper mines which were, at that time, the main source of income for the country. There I was met by my friend Rose's parents, Dr David and Rosanna Kaye. Previously missionaries working at Kalene Mission, they were by then living and working in Luanshya. From there I was given a lift by a local trader. He was driving a heavily laden lorry with seven tons of supplies being transported westwards to 'our' area of Zambia. The journey that time took three days over the very poor dirt roads, stopping overnight at different missions.

I had been afraid of not understanding God's guidance, making mistakes and concerned that it might be my desire as opposed to God's plan. But, as explained, He dealt with that in ways that left me so sure this new life was in His plan for me. It meant that in the future years, when some things were really tough, I could say to Him – You brought me here so You have to deal with it!

After making the decision to return and work there, it was confirmed again and again, by fellow missionaries, and by the elders of my home church who had in the same mail received a letter about the need for a nurse there and another from me saying I believed it right to go to Lukolwe.

And so began the next twenty-five years ... being taught by a Father who does not waste any experience. I faced challenges and failure, but experienced the joy of knowing His love even at the lowest times.

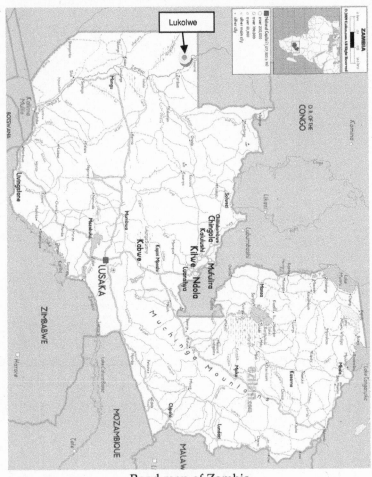

Road map of Zambia
©2009 Ezilon.com road map of Zambia (accessed 10th August 2013).

LUKOLWE
1965-1990

Lukolwe is a very isolated area in the north-west corner of Zambia. It is situated 550 miles (885km) due west of the Copperbelt towns of Chingola, Kitwe and Ndola and surrounding areas. Then after crossing the Zambezi River there are a further ten miles of rough sandy tracks to even reach it. It had begun as a residential mission in 1958 although missionaries had been visiting the area for many years. Chavuma Mission is only fifteen miles away, but across (east of) the Zambezi River, which had no bridges, and the journey there often took at least two hours, and on occasion might take a whole, long, demanding day.

The mighty Zambezi River is born as a small spring in the Mwinilunga area of Zambia's North-Western Province, close to Kalene Mission. It runs west into Angola, growing steadily. Then it meanders due south back into Zambia and as far as the

Victoria Falls near Livingstone. From there it runs eastward along the border between Zambia and Zimbabwe, through Lake Kariba and the Cahora Bassa Dam and onwards through Mozambique to the Indian Ocean.

It is the fourth longest river in Africa, covering 2,700km. By the time it re-enters Zambia at Chavuma, where we crossed it, it is a fast-flowing dangerous river up to 400m wide in the rainy season. To the west it cuts off a strip the length of Zambia about 100–150km (ninety miles) wide and Lukolwe is in the northern part of that strip. There are no road bridges at all across this mighty river from Cazombo in Angola (well north of the border) right through to Victoria Falls at Livingstone, in the south.

First impressions

During the visit I had some impressions of the place and the life of the area, but it was only when living there permanently that those impressions were strengthened, or in some cases had to be changed radically.

At that time, 1965, there were six missionaries based at Lukolwe. The residential work had started seven years earlier when elderly Mr Bert Sims, his son John, daughter-in-law Eleanor and their family, were joined by Lorne and Betty Lou Ferguson and their four boys from California, and David Croudace from Rhodesia. Lorne was a Bible teacher, but also a very practical person whose skills were invaluable through the years. Lorne and David had some medical training prior to arrival, and the two ladies had learned skills on the job.

Mr Sims had developed terminal cancer and lived for only a few months after I arrived at Lukolwe, David moved down to Zambezi Township to work with the youth in the secondary school and John Sims' family left in 1970 for the education of their children. Although during the years that followed a few young couples joined us, none stayed very long as they found the isolation and lifestyle too hard.

On the visit I had stayed in Mr Sims' metal-roofed bedsit, but he returned a few months later needing his own home. Meanwhile John and Eleanor had moved out of their old empty mud-brick house into their much more comfortable newly built home. I was allowed to use part of the old building.

The old mud house was what it sounds like, made of mud, and the termites thoroughly enjoyed building their nests in the walls, the curtains, or on and through anything I might carelessly leave lying on the floor. They are amazing creatures as they can destroy the contents of a cardboard box and leave it looking externally intact. Basically they leave only an extremely thin layer of paper on the outside of a sand construction which replaces the previous contents and cardboard.

The house had a corrugated iron roof, no ceilings, and a bare cement floor. The wind howled through the 18in gap between the top of the walls and the metal roofing, and sometimes the rain too, but I was grateful to have somewhere to make my home.

The lack of water or sanitation was rather more of a problem. Later Lorne fitted a bathroom handbasin indoors, with running cold water. The bath was a tin tub about a metre long, and had to be emptied by baling it out and pouring the water down the basin plughole, which had a drainage pipe to a channel on the outside. A small water pipe came from outside through the wall and ended above where the bath tub would be placed. It produced hot water, if and when the 'volcano' water heating system had been lit. The 'volcano' was a container about 15cm diameter and maybe 45cm high. It had a thin metal water pipe curled around inside it, and the central space left was then filled with small twigs and a fire lit. This heated the water running through the pipe which then protruded through the wall to supply the bath. Cold water, if needed, was added from a bucket.

On one memorable occasion, after bathing I baled out the bath tub and picked it up to drain the last of the water. Looking over the top I saw a small snake. Apparently the snake had enjoyed the cool damp beneath the tin tub and curled up comfortably. When I poured water into the tub, the snake was trapped by the weight, made worse when I climbed in as well! I was very thankful to realise that it was well and truly dead.

Toilet arrangements were simpler – a bucket with a toilet seat on a wooden frame was placed behind a curtain at the end of the open rear veranda. The bucket had to be emptied daily down the deep long-drop latrine some way from the house.

I lived there for several years. As it was not possible for me to cook a main meal in the mud house, the two families kindly alternated in inviting me to many and varied daily meals, for which I was grateful.

Although content with the house and managing well, an incident involving a visitor threw it up in a different light. The lady visitor seemed to enjoy her time with us, staying in the guest accommodation of one family and having the freedom to roam around. But when she returned to her home town and visited my parents, she declared that mine was the 'worst missionary housing' she had ever seen. This naturally did not go down well with either my parents or the local church, and became very embarrassing.

Several years later we employed Bill Collias, whom I had first met at Balovale airport on my initial visit, to build a more substantial hospital ward block for inpatients. While with us he generously insisted that he would also build me a house, using plans I had already drawn up and the corrugated iron roofing sheets my father had had sent from Salisbury some time before. The new house was built of cement blocks, plastered, had ceilings, etc. There I really enjoyed the cleanliness, plumbing, ceilings and having my own bathroom and kitchen. At the time of building, Bill knew that I did not have enough money to pay for the finished work, but persisted in building the house anyway, with the agreement that I could pay him the balance whenever I could afford it. It was another step of faith for me to accept a friend's generosity, as I had made it a principle never to go into debt. The house was paid off completely over the next five years.

What a difference that home meant to me, and then later to others who shared it with me, or used it after I finally left Lukolwe.

A new name

Very soon after moving to Lukolwe, the local Christians gave me a new name, a Luvale name. Hopeful of the help my medical training would prove to be, they named me 'Samba', meaning 'to justify'. From that time onwards, throughout my time in Zambia, I was known as Samba, or the more polite form of 'Ndona Samba' (a respectful title). The name was given with affection and I soon learned to love and appreciate the Luvale people among whom I lived and worked.

Although my training in nursing and midwifery had been good, and with considerable experience, the community there saw it differently. The first baby I delivered at Lukolwe was a little girl, and all through the years that followed she was known proudly by her family as 'the very first baby Samba ever, ever delivered'. In later years it was a joy to care for her when she gave birth to her own children too.

During those first few months we had a tragedy in the hospital that really challenged me. My language learning was still elementary, but enough for me to have been able to care for a young mother in labour with her first baby. Baby was born safely and the mother was delighted with her. After caring for the mother and dressing the baby, we moved them out into the maternity ward. There were no beds at that time and patients used their own straw mats on the floor, but they were used to that and were quite comfortable.

Shortly after returning to my house there was frantic clapping outside (clapping was the equivalent of knocking on the door) and I could understand enough to know they were saying, 'Come quickly, come quickly.' Running back to the hospital several hundred yards away, I was shocked to see a limp mother lying on her mat. Apparently, when we were able to sort out the language barrier, etc, it turned out that she had seemed fine, then suddenly sat up on the mat and fell backwards, dead. It was as sudden as that. Very possibly she had had a pulmonary embolus (clot on the lung), but there was nothing more we could do for her. Thankfully, I was never again to see that complication after delivery, but at the time it shook me to the core. It also meant that we had the small orphan baby (cared for by her grandmother) living with us at the hospital for about a year until she was fully weaned and strong enough to manage back in the village without the milk we'd supplied. I still marvel that there did not seem to be any backlash as a result of my being a newcomer and 'so inexperienced', as the community saw it.

Not only was the culture new, but new seasons of the year affected daily life in ways not experienced before.

During the dry season from about May to August it was cool and pleasant. It would be cold in the early mornings (on one remembered occasion in a girls' camp we broke thick ice on the top of a bucket of water), but by about 9am we were warm enough to wear short-sleeved cotton dresses. It rained extremely rarely during those months and we could plan ahead. The Zambezi River water level also dropped to its lowest, making the crossing easier.

During September the days grew hotter, the humidity increasing as the approaching rains began to build in intensity. September and October were very hot and muggy. Then when the first rains fell we would often go outside and just revel in the smell of the earth and the feel of the rain on our faces.

From then through to April, thunderstorms would be common, often coming late each afternoon. The huge plains over a wide area would flood, fish eggs hidden in the dry ground would hatch, and it was a time of plenty for the people around as they caught and dried the fish, ate their fill of fish and fruits, and generally replenished their poorly nourished bodies.

During the first few months I was there, another tragedy occurred in the hospital. Betty Lou and I had gone over to the maternity room to discharge a new baby and his mother. We spent a little time with the mother and gave them the gifts of little sweaters and woollen blankets, sent out in containers from the UK by Medical Missionary News. (Based in Essex, they support medical missionaries and hospitals in their work in various parts of the world. To us their work was greatly valued.) My language skills were still minimal so Betty Lou was with me and had the insight to take an umbrella. Suddenly there was very heavy rain and a crash of thunder and it was as though someone had punched me in the back and thrown me across the room. By the time I was rising to my feet there was shouting outside, 'Come quickly, Noah has been hit.'

The rainwater was more than ankle-deep as we ran across to the ward in which Noah had been sitting with his back to the wall, his wife on a mat beside him, and his newborn baby in a small wooden cot at their feet. The lightning had struck the corrugated iron roof in that set of rooms, passed down a hardwood pole in the wall and entered the back of Noah's head. It had also broken off a piece of wood from the window frame about 30cm (12in) long and with an exceedingly sharp point at one end. The wood must have spun with power about 2m through the air and was lodged point-first through the baby's blankets, between his legs and into the mattress below. The baby was unharmed but his father had been killed outright by the lightning strike. Throughout the row of ten small wards, shocked people had minor injuries from burns on their fingers where they had been touching metal beds, etc.

Relieved that the baby was safe, it was an introduction to the wailing associated with death, but also to the response of so many people around. Apparently Noah had been notoriously one of the most promiscuous men in the area. He lived in the village right on the edge of the mission grounds, and for all those involved there was no peace, the witchdoctor drummed all night and the community mourned a man who was lost for all eternity.

What a contrast it was to the deaths of some of the Christians with which I was involved later. That thunderstorm stands out as perhaps the most devastating of many storms experienced during the years ahead.

Although the missionaries had longed for a nurse to ease the demands of the medical work, it is human nature not always to enjoy the consequences of change. For some folk it was hard to hand over the medical work. After a period of introducing me to that work and the language, which must have actually increased the demands on their time, there came the point when it was right for them to step back and allow the 'new nurse' to manage in her way, asking and receiving help with language and so on as needed. But for one person in particular there were other aspects to caring for the people medically which were harder to relinquish. It freed up her time considerably and she still had a great deal of other involvement in the lives of the community, but there were areas of power and of day-to-day contact which were lost. Probably, suffering feelings of real frustration at times, I was not as sensitive to this as I should have been. Looking back from this distance, I can see the picture even more clearly, but at the time it was far from easy for either of us.

Gradually we began to settle down into the new routines, but I still had so much to learn. Medically, I had been trained to high standards of sterility, etc. Thankfully, during the latter part of my midwifery training and for the months I worked as a district midwife, I had learned the concept of cleanliness as opposed to sterility as we handled instruments. After use, the equipment was all sterilised, but then packed away in our little midwifery suitcases, clean and ready for the next time. At Lukolwe the staff in the hospital had no concept of germs, or of sterility, and, trying to teach them, I was the one frustrated by it all. A microscope showed them some of the germs. Even so, the concept of cleanliness was easier than that of absolute sterility. We had to come to a balance of what was achievable for the staff, most of whom had only had three to four years of rural primary schooling. Of course, this would not have been satisfactory if we had had a doctor, or were doing surgery, but in the context in which we worked it was effective, and I cannot remember any in-house infections developing.

Living at Lukolwe threw me into a very different lifestyle. Except among my expatriate fellow workers, virtually no English was spoken. When first there, various acceptable 'rules of conduct' had been explained to me by a senior missionary, such as never to be seen wearing trousers, be very careful in all contact with missionaries of the opposite gender because the local population would be hypercritical, etc. This made it particularly difficult for those of us who were single, increased the feeling of aloneness, and basically meant that we could never fully relax even when visiting on other mission stations.

When I was at Capernwray Bible School there had been one particularly close friend and we had discussed the possibility that we might have shared our lives together. At that time God was leading me to a life and work in Zambia, and my friend was returning home to another continent. We never met again, although we corresponded for a while. Some time after my going to Lukolwe he wanted to visit, but I refused to let him, out of fear – fear of others' reactions, of the local people's response, of the 'rules' I had been given when first there – and, probably most of all, out of a deep unrecognised inner response which I would only understand many years later. Sometimes I have wondered how different the future might have been if he had made that visit.

The commitment to go to Lukolwe had not been a commitment to singleness per se, so that particular aspect of life had to be handed back to the Lord many times through the years. Days were busy, demands were plentiful and life was fulfilling but, too, there could be times of loneliness and a longing for close and personal companionship.

Perhaps even more difficult was the steep learning curve involved in immersion in a new culture. Besides the learning of spoken Luvale, people's body language was different, so it was dangerous to try to read from the signs they seemed to give when not understanding what they had said. Thankfully, the Luvale people are kind and considerate, willing to teach if one wanted to learn, and reached out to help.

Relationships were not always easy, not only with local folk, but also with my fellow missionaries who were from different backgrounds too, and therefore in so many ways this was yet another culture. I must have seemed different to them as well, I suppose!

Within the local community there was the danger of people responding in ways they thought would most please me or the people to whom they were speaking. This often caused confusion. I can well remember, many years after going to Lukolwe, when an English-speaking Indian government doctor from the nearest hospital, more than sixty miles and a river crossing away, came with his interpreter to visit a local village area. They were talking about training health workers to be based in the village. Having been invited to attend the meeting, I was sitting in the crowd and it was a very interesting lesson to understand clearly both languages and how the translation matched or, as in this case, did not match the doctor's words. At one point the doctor clearly stated that such a health worker would not be supplied with any medicines. The translation came through with words that deeply pleased the people listening: 'The health worker would be supplied with medicines.' At that point it was necessary for me to interrupt and clarify the situation. By then I was an accepted and trusted member of the community, so those around appreciated the intervention but were very disappointed. They tried to argue with the doctor, who remained adamant. If the words had not been corrected, the repercussions would have rebounded on us in the mission medical work at a later date. When the government hospital had not supplied the longed-for medicines, the local population would have expected me to fulfil the 'promise' from the medicines we used in our medical work, not an abundant supply. Taking on misunderstood government commitments was not our forte!

Cross-cultural issues were challenging. In October 1990, after my return to the UK, I was on the editorial committee for *Footsteps* magazine, a Tearfund production devoted to health, medical and basic issues to promote healthy living, particularly in rural areas of the world. I replied to one letter received regarding traditional cultural issues and the article shows clearly other areas of learning as we relate to different and new cultures. See Appendix 1.

Language study

Language learning had never been easy for me, although I had studied Afrikaans up to matriculation level and used it during my nursing training in Cape Town. I was more inclined to maths than languages. My learning of Latin in school had been one of the few areas of total failure, partly owing to the frequent changes of teachers and teaching methods. Interestingly, much imbibed in those Latin lessons stood me in good stead later when studying medicinal terminology. Learning a new language is never easy, and for some people particularly difficult.

When I went to Lukolwe I had no choice but to immerse myself in the Luvale language. With the exception of my fellow missionaries, no one in the area spoke English and I had fully expected to be involved in language study. Yet I still believe the skills and ability to learn to speak Luvale well were a special God-given gift, enabling communication with the people on many levels.

Mr Albert Horton of Angola had prepared a grammar of Luvale, and later a dictionary.[10] These tools were

---

[10] Albert E Horton, *A Grammar of Luvale* (Johannesburg: Witwatersrand University Press, Bantu Grammatical Archives, 1949); and *A Dictionary*

available and through the years became invaluable. The only problem was that the dictionary was only a translation from Luvale into English. For good reasons we did not have an English to Luvale version. Both the grammar and the dictionary were also written at a university thesis level and were excellent productions. But for the newcomer to the language, it did not feel simple enough! In the beginning I often found that an Oxford English Dictionary was needed for me to understand the language of the grammar. Thankfully, much later, he also prepared a more basic lesson guide[11] for the total beginner.

Early on, as I continued to study, I began to hear what was said more than understanding the complicated grammar with all its prefixes and multiple suffixes for every verb. In the area of medical work, communication became possible fairly quickly, but outside that limited day-to-day vocabulary my language skills were minimal. Onomatopoeia plays a huge role in the Luvale language. It creates a sound effect that mimics the thing described, making the description more expressive and interesting. This can be helpful, but is sometimes hilarious when attempted by the newcomer. At Lukolwe we had the privilege of living in an area with only one basic Bantu language, which was a great help. At least one other fairly local mission had a population that spoke up to five

of *Luvale* (Angola, 1953, revised 1975 [no other publication details shown – probably as above]).
[11] Albert E Horton, *Graded Lessons in Luvale* (Tracy City, TN, 1979).

different Bantu languages, making language learning much more complicated.

An example of some of the complexities of the language may be shown with the simple word 'love'. Love as a noun was *'zangi'*. As a verb it became *'-zanga'*. That was basic memorisation, but the verb then had prefixes and suffixes added to give tenses and even nuances very much more expressive than in English.

Kuzanga	to love
Ngunazange	I love
Ngunamizange	I love you
Ngwamizangilanga	I loved you – in the recent past
Ngwamizangilililanga	I have loved you (long-term) and will go on doing so …

… and so it went on.

Even nouns were not straightforward. For instance, a dog was *'kawa'*, but beginning with a 'u', as *'uwa'* meant the concept of being a dog – how a dog would act and behave, 'doginess', etc. These were often concepts not expressed in English and were applied to a wide range of objects and attitudes.

After about a year I felt I was doing fairly well and continued to progress in communication with people of that local community, mainly with hospital-based vocabulary. Then after about five years I started going out into village areas for one or two nights a month. As I sat among the local villagers and became part of the group in their outside thatched kitchens, it was with the realisation that I could understand very little indeed! That was when I gradually began to hear what was going on around me. One-to-one communication on subjects I understood had been fine, but sitting in a group and hearing the chatter around me was more challenging. Only then did I really begin to understand and appreciate the language and people in which I was immersed. Probably it was only much later, when I was encouraging and supporting other newcomers in language study, that the actual grammar made sense. Many people can learn a language by studying grammar books, but for others it is learned far more effectively through hearing and absorbing the intonations and grammatical constructions, without necessarily understanding the rules behind them all. It took many years before it became natural to pray in Luvale, or even dream in that language.

Through the years I became fluent in more colloquial Luvale, with clarity of understanding and an ability to communicate with the people around me, rather than in the full grammatical sense. It was a privilege the first time that I was referred to as a 'kaLuvale', or one of the Luvale people. This came about mainly from my ability to hear the nuances of the language, despite my poor accent. The Luvale people were amazingly generous in their encouragement of anyone who wanted to learn to speak their language, and spent many hours teaching me words and meanings and encouraging my curiosity.

One time when we were in the maternity room awaiting the birth of a baby, the patient's grandmother came into the room holding a stick about 45cm (18in) long. On the end of the stick clung a huge hairy spider which she then proceeded to poke across the top of the bed over the labouring mother and into my face. As she did so she kept on repeating the word '*kalumbukamukala*', meaning tarantula. Now, spiders have never been very popular with me and this particular one, if it had been standing on the floor, would probably have covered the size of a small plate. I had also heard that tarantulas were poisonous and could jump some considerable distance, so having this furry ball within inches of my face was terrifying. Thankfully, the poor creature, stuck on the end of a small stick, had no choice to do anything but hang on tightly. It was finally put outside. I had learned a new word, as had been the purpose of the whole exercise. The young mother seemed completely unfazed by the experience and went on to give birth to a healthy little baby.

Knowing my desire to learn I was brought many items, including dead snakes and other creatures, to be taught what they were called. The dictionary came into its own when my friends brought me unusual items, with their Luvale names spoken loudly to enable my (restricted?) hearing. The notebook I carried was filled with new words, and sometimes repeats of the ones I already knew, as someone insisted that I had to 'write it down'.

Medical work

Much of the medical work was routine ... depending on your definition of routine! It certainly was not the routine of a large hospital in any country, particularly a Western one. We were isolated. At best, the nearest doctor was five hours' journey away across the Zambezi River.

Every day was different. In theory we all met ready to start work at seven o'clock each morning. Some days we would start with a meeting with the staff; once weekly to look at the Scriptures together; another morning for teaching them about the medical work. Our staff, for most of my stay in Zambia, were local people who had had a very few years at school. The 'Dressers' – I do not know the origin of the name – were the ones who cared for the patients, and all were reasonably literate in their own language. They did an amazing job, and learned to diagnose and treat many common ailments, when to call for more help, etc. In the early years I was on call twenty-four hours a day and an undisturbed night of sleep was rare. But as time went by, the Dressers and the nurse in maternity were able to cope with many more aspects of the work without needing support, considerably improving my sleep patterns.

The staff would then begin their early-morning routines. I'd start in the pharmacy, filling the containers with the stock medicines they needed and preparing any necessary home-made remedies we were using. Besides the cost, basic medicines were not easy to obtain. Medical Missionary News supplied us with considerable quantities of them and we were always grateful, but the supplies they sent still all had to be transported the 885km in from the Copperbelt.

Then would follow rounds of all the inpatients, before commencing whatever outpatients' clinic was arranged for that day. This all sounds smoothly routine, but it seldom worked that way. The outside workmen might have arrived wanting some instructions or help, or a mother was in labour in the maternity room and so on. Each Thursday we set off at about 7am, drove an hour or more to the village area for that week's children's and antenatal clinics, and often were not back until late afternoon or early evening. Once a month, the week of the waxing moon, we would leave on a Friday morning for clinics in more distant areas, spending two nights and returning on Sunday afternoon. The evening moonlight meant we could see without any lighting, which made life more pleasant.

Our patients basically relied on one form of transport – their own feet. Many walked for long distances, and during crises their friends would carry them in to us slung in a blanket hanging from a pole, or pushing the patient on a bicycle. The Ferguson family and I had the only two vehicles in that whole area west of the Zambezi River and there was no possibility of providing on-demand 'ambulance' facilities. People understandably would have really liked us to provide such transport for them, but limited resources and physical strength made that impossible.

Village clinic.

After discussion with local community leaders, it was realised that either I could be available for care of those already in the hospital, or be constantly rushing back and forth to transport those who requested it. But cultural expectations came into the picture as well, and it was not easy. Eventually it was accepted that I could not go out and collect all patients who sent in messages asking for that service, but if they were brought in to us and then consequently needed further urgent transportation to a doctor, we would provide that care.

It was hard to have to say 'No' to anxious relatives pleading for us to go out for their patient, and was another way in which I learned to rely on the Holy Spirit's prompting in my heart. Several times through the years I had initially, as routine, refused to go out to someone asking for help. But then, after the disappointed relatives had left, I had a deep conviction that I should indeed go. That meant ensuring the vehicle had sufficient fuel and was ready to go, grabbing my emergency medical bag and then driving in the direction the relatives had indicated. Each time I had that inner conviction it proved to have been an essential journey.

Balancing the demands placed upon us, unrealistic expectations, personal and physical strength, the needs of the patients already on site, broken nights, etc, was always challenging, and resulted in a clash of cultures on a number of occasions. It was so easy, particularly when I was tired, to feel that my way was the right one and the requests being made unreasonable (from my point of view!). Through the years we had to learn to unknot the resulting tangle of opinions and resentments and at times to apologise to one another.

Maternity work

Through the years at Lukolwe the maternity work grew steadily, and usually we also held antenatal clinics when out weighing babies and immunising all children in the remote villages. The vast majority of mothers gave birth safely, although there were fairly often complications which we would not have handled in the Western world. In the 1970s, when visiting my mother in Salisbury (later Harare), I had worked in a large advanced obstetric hospital for six weeks, being trained in the care of obstetric emergencies and obstructed labour. As a result, I acquired the ability to perform a symphisiotomy – surgery on the pelvis, which also results in the pelvis being permanently larger than before, thus making future pregnancies safer. It can sometimes save the need for a caesarean for obstructed labour, but also has inherent serious dangers for the mother if mishandled.

On one occasion when relatives asked for me to go and collect a patient, I initially refused. As they walked off, an inner response prompted me to follow them in the Land Cruiser. The patient, a first-time teenage mother in labour, was only about a mile away. When I found her she looked fine, and apparently cheerfully climbed up into the back of the pickup without help. My inner reaction was to feel the trip had been unnecessary when she was so close to the hospital. Imagine my shock, shortly after moving her into the maternity room and examining her, to find that she was in life-threatening obstructed labour. In labour, she had walked almost thirty miles to reach us, and finally just told her relatives she could go no further. She made no fuss, and just accepted the situation.

Ideally she would have needed a caesarean section to deliver the baby, but the journey to a doctor would take too long. Thankfully, because of the special skills in which I had been trained, it was possible to help her immediately by doing a symphisiotomy, and the result was a healthy mother and baby. That was one person who desperately needed the transport, and the help we could give, and I am sure that it was the Holy Spirit who prompted me to change my mind that day.

Several years later, the Zambian Minister for Health, accompanied by the country's senior obstetrician, flew up on a surprise visit from Lusaka. They came in a huge army helicopter, landing on our grass airstrip at Lukolwe. It was a Sunday, and this entourage arrived out of the blue. I was recovering from a bout of malaria and still in bed when someone arrived to tell me the visitors were arriving at the house. It is amazing how quickly one can rise and dress when the need arises! Kettles were boiled, pancakes made, and they were all served refreshments.

When the obstetrician asked me about the symphisiotomies I was fully expecting to be told off for poor medical practice. After all, I was not a doctor! But instead he was full of praise and had chosen to make the journey to give me encouragement in the work we were doing. Amazing! How had he even heard about it?

Skills learned were very beneficial to many of the women we treated. But perhaps the most difficult situation was with one particular maternity patient, in the mid 1980s. A lady we knew well came into the maternity unit from a distant village. She had several other children and this pregnancy had felt 'different', so she had come in earlier than usual. On the way, she had begun to experience severe pain. When I examined her it was clear that she was in labour, but also in agonisingly abnormal pain. She was not only carrying twins, but doing so in a critical situation, whereby she was bleeding internally as at least part of the placenta had begun to separate from the wall of the womb. We were facing an extreme and life-threatening situation and on that occasion there was, once again, no possibility of transporting her to a doctor as the Zambezi River was not crossable. In addition we were not set up to perform a caesarean section, which could possibly have saved the mother's life.

None of the staff, including myself, had ever seen this problem, although Nicki (a young Registered Nurse and midwife who had come out from England – more about her later) and I had learned about it during training days. We both knew it was a genuine life-threatening emergency. After prayer, and a searching of medical textbooks, as well as monitoring the patient, we realised that she urgently needed a blood transfusion. Of course, we had no blood in the fridge, or even a full laboratory to cross-match accurately. While Nicki anxiously cared for the very ill mother, I went round her relatives trying to persuade them to donate blood. This was a new concept to them, and carried with it the inherent danger that if the patient still died, the person giving the blood might then be blamed for the death as a result of their 'bad' blood. After discussing this with them for some time, permission was finally given to take samples to try to cross-match their blood with the patient. Many years before, I had helped in the Red Cross blood transfusion service (as a young teenager) and I had seen and later read about a basic cross-matching that used to be used, whereby red cells from the donated blood were mixed with the serum of the recipient then checked under a microscope to see whether the red cells agglutinated (clumped together) or not. It was basic. It was dangerous. But unless we did something, we were certainly going to lose the mother as well as her babies.

Finding two people whose blood seemed compatible, we took a pint from each of them and gave it to the mother. The fresh blood transfusion seemed to strengthen the mother adequately and allow her blood to clot sufficiently to overcome the internal bleeding. Thankfully, she showed no negative side effects from the transfusions. The contractions she was experiencing strengthened and we were able to deliver the two stillborn babies. Then it was possible to treat the bleeding. That very ill lady needed a considerable time to recover her strength, but was able to return to her village and care for her large family. How we praised the Lord for His protection and enabling.

Working together

Looking through my journals of the days at Lukolwe, I came across a batch from 1978–83. During that period, a young nurse came to join in the work, particularly in the hospital. With hindsight, it is easy to see that she had personal issues that made it very difficult for her to live and work in that environment. Up to that time, I had been the only qualified member of the medical staff. It seemed as though, at last, there was going to be someone with whom to share the workload. My initial response was real joy, but it proved to be a very difficult five years. Helen was a trained nurse and midwife and had a good ear for learning Luvale, so progressed well in her language understanding.

She found life difficult in many ways, and was unable to carry a fair share of the responsibility. I personally struggled throughout that time, often feeling a failure as it did not seem possible to relate well to her. Oh, the personal struggles revealed in those journal entries. And yet, from this distance, remembering back to those days, and rereading what is written, I am still astonished at the answers to prayer and the insightful wisdom given at the time.

For eighteen months the Ferguson family were back in the United States and Helen and I were left as the only residential expatriates in the whole area. It was a huge responsibility made considerably more difficult by our isolation on that west side of the Zambezi River. All the responsibility for the hospital, transport of patients and supplies essentially rested on me and my knowledge of the environment.

Through the years there have been many times when I have felt at the end of my tether, for whatever reason, and wanted out of a particular situation – because life as it was just seemed too hard. Then, in my daily reading I would perhaps read Paul's admonishment to Timothy:

> Endure hardship with us like a good soldier of Christ Jesus. No-one serving as a soldier gets involved in civilian affairs – he wants to please his commanding officer.
>
> (2 Timothy 2:3-4, NIV 1984)

Somehow that put me back on track to say, 'Yes, Lord, I will go on.' That was so true during those months.

For three months of the time another nurse/midwife, Ruth, joined us. She came because she believed that a God of discipline was sending her to Lukolwe as a punishment for things that had previously 'gone wrong' in her Christian life. Learning this as we travelled up from South Africa together in a new Toyota Land Cruiser I had just collected, my prayer for her was that during her stay with us she would begin to know God as a God of love. Life was not easy, and so often it seemed to me that there was no way that prayer was to be fulfilled. Yet some time after she had left Lukolwe, Ruth wrote to me:

> Quite early in my appointment five years ago I showed a friend the photos of my trip with you up to Zambia, especially of Lukolwe. What a culture shock it was for me and how you cared for my every need and looked after me so well. On looking back, what a privilege it was for me to be with you there and see firsthand all the fruit of your years of serving Jesus at Lukolwe.

Ruth had been in Cape Town for her nursing training, and she arrived in the UK to train as a midwife. We – Rose with whom I had travelled to England, and myself – met up with her during our midwifery training in London and Exeter, then Ruth and I went to Capernwray Bible School together. It was thirty-nine years later that she wrote to me about our time together, and her comments were challenging and humbling:

> Every time I give my testimony of how I came to put my trust in Jesus as Saviour and Lord, I speak of your kind befriending of me at Guy's and through midwifery and Capernwray. To see the fruit of the Holy Spirit and character of Jesus in your lives through that year of being born again, quite overwhelmed me. I was witnessing the very life of Jesus in you all and this has stayed with me all these years. My fervent

prayer has always been that I might also show the same beautiful character of Jesus in my life too.[12]

That Christmas (1982) was particularly difficult. Usually all the Christians in the area spent Christmas Day together as members of the church. There would be a long, relaxed and joyous service throughout the morning (all in Luvale), followed by eating a meal together. The huge *shima* (a heavy, almost solid 'porridge' made of cassava meal, maize meal, meal from bulrush millet or a mixture of these), with locally sourced meat, leaves and probably beans, would be prepared by some of the local women in massive pots over open fires. Spreading out a huge tarpaulin, we would all sit around in small groups and eat with our fingers from the communal dishes. For the local Christians it was a time of fun, laughter and worship. It also allowed them respite from work and from the intense drinking and revelry in the villages around.

Understandably, neither Helen nor Ruth found such a long day easy. The language was foreign and local food felt scarcely palatable, so they did not look forward to the day. We had prepared ourselves a special meal on Christmas Eve and made that our time of personal sharing. In addition I suggested that the three of us should all go off to the Zambezi River for a picnic on Boxing Day. I went ahead with the preparations and early on 26th December prepared the picnic, then went to the

---

[12] Extracts from letters from Ruth written in 2002. Used with permission.

hospital to make a round of all the patients, and to check with the staff regarding supplies. On the way, the Land Cruiser needed checking for sufficient fuel, tyres, etc. The accoutrements for safe use of the boat had to be packed into the back of the vehicle, including paddles, keys, fuel for the outboard and so on.

By about 8am I was walking back towards the house when I heard the sound of a vehicle approaching. That was so rare, and particularly on a bank holiday, when the government pontoon was not operating, so my curiosity was raised. Imagine my surprise when a Land Rover pulled up beside me and five smiling faces beamed out. Cheerful voices announced that they thought we might be lonely over Christmas so had come to spend the day with us, and had brought their own picnic. It was four of the sisters/nuns and a young Father from the Catholic mission thirty miles south of us. They had left at 5am in order to make the three-hour journey over very rough tracks.

When they heard that we were preparing to go out for a day on the river, they were delighted to join us. Our outboard motorboat was plenty large enough to take us all. Both Ruth and Helen joined in as well, and we had such a special and refreshing day out. We boated down the Zambezi River as far as a pleasant sandbank and stopped for a picnic. The day was glorious, with no rain even though it was the rainy season. It was wonderful to have fresh people with whom to chat in our own language and we all thoroughly enjoyed the day. Then our five visitors had to set off on their long journey home.

Personally I felt that it was just another evidence of God's loving care shown when it was most needed.

Partly as a result of the experience with Helen, I had come to the conclusion that, in our situation, accepting a short-term expatriate worker meant an enormously increased workload for me. Therefore I would not encourage anyone in such a capacity, even if they offered. It is hard to describe the intensity and pressure that such mentoring had added to our daily living.

However, after Helen left us in early 1983, I really struggled. The Ferguson family, who had returned after eighteen months away, were talking about the possibility of a permanent return to the States for the education of their family. It would have meant that I would have to carry on as the only expatriate, with all that was involved in life and living in that remote place. Maintaining the fabric of buildings, vehicles for supplies and emergencies was physically demanding, without the medical calls and other emotionally draining demands of each day.

It was in the middle of August 1983 and another long evening spent on my knees talking it over with the Lord. Towards midnight there came a time where I cried out, 'Please let me out of here, it is too hard and I do not want to go on struggling any more.' There were tears and sobbing, but there came a point where I was able to hand it all back to the Lord with the cry, 'I will stay here if that is what You want.' I was willing to stay, whatever the cost might be, until He showed me His plan. Then came something I have never experienced before – or since. There, sitting on my bed inside the mosquito net 'tent' it felt as though I was wrapped in a great big soft warm blanket of love. It was something so real and tangible that it brought security and peace. I knew and felt God's presence in a very special way.

Tumba

The Ferguson family later made the decision to stay on at Lukolwe, and life continued for the next few months. Then in early November, out of the blue – or rather the very slow postal system – came a letter from Nicki Keen. Nicki was a young, newly trained Registered Nurse, enquiring as to whether she could come out as a short-term worker for six months prior to commencing her midwifery training. She had been given our contact details through Medical Missionary News. As the Fergusons and I prayed about it, I felt sure it was right to invite her to join us despite my previous reluctance, and replied by return of mail. Remembering my own experience when first visiting Lukolwe, we arranged that all future contacts would be through the two-way radio system, as our 'return of mail' took a minimum of six weeks in those days. Of course we had no telephones at all and even telegrams might take many weeks to reach us, if they ever did.

Within four weeks Nicki flew from London to Ndola airport on the Zambian Copperbelt, where I met her. We began the journey back to Lukolwe the following day, staying overnight with friends at Chizera Mission (Africa Evangelical Fellowship) on the way. Thus began a relationship that was to prove to be one of God's *'exceeding abundances'* (see Ephesians 3:20, KJV) for me over the following months, and in fact for all the years since then.

Nicki came with a heart filled with love for the people around her. She came prepared to work at language study, despite it being for a short term only. She was willing to turn her hand to any challenge and hungry to learn and grow.

The people of the community loved her from the beginning and gave her the name 'Tumba', from a Luvale proverb 'Kwalivanga Samba Tumba keshi kutonda chihelako' (saying that Samba – myself – came first and therefore Tumba did not have to look for a place to settle). We worked together in the medical work and complemented one another. Nicki challenged me on many fronts as her interest in everything resulted in constant questions. One of the areas of challenge was why we worked as we did (so often non-standard from a UK hospital point of view). At first it felt a little threatening, but I soon began to enjoy the challenge, although often had to reply, 'I do not know right now, but give me time to think it through and I'll let you know.' In all truth, some of the adaptations we had made had challenged me in my early years, but we had gradually found satisfactory ways around the different issues. Through the years the changed ways had become habitual, and it felt good to look at them anew.

Nicki became a special friend, and as we lived in the same home and worked together, the relationship grew. Also, Nicki was there for me through a particularly difficult six months of my life. Another blessing was that Nicki later returned to Lukolwe, after completing her midwifery training, and we worked together for a number of years. She stayed on for a time even after I had returned to England. Through the years our friendship has grown and now, back in England, she lives with her husband and family only about a mile away from my home.

Family

God's plans are made in wonderful ways at times, although sometimes as we experience them they do not necessarily feel like blessings!

At the end of March 1973 I developed an eye problem that needed attention. The only doctor in the area was the government doctor in Zambezi Township, sixty miles away across the Zambezi River. When I went down to see him, he was puzzled, but felt that there could be a serious problem, so presented me with return air tickets to fly down to Lusaka to see the most senior eye specialist in Zambia. Arriving in Lusaka, I visited that highly respected specialist's clinic and he in turn felt unable to accurately diagnose what potentially might be a very serious condition, and referred me on to a specialist consultant in Salisbury, Rhodesia. Again I was presented with free return air tickets for the flight to Salisbury!

Meanwhile, although concerned about the work I had so abruptly left at Lukolwe, I gratefully accepted that the trip to Salisbury, another 1,600km away, would give me some unexpected time staying with my parents. The day after my arrival there, I had an appointment with the consultant. Within a mere five minutes he diagnosed a viral condition, causing easily seen small ulcers on the cornea, and he showed me illustrations of the condition. It needed no further treatment except time and eye drops to ease the irritation. Surprised, relieved and rather embarrassed, I discussed it with my parents and booked a flight back to Zambia for a week later. Initially I was really puzzled, but in retrospect came to realise that God must have 'blinded' the eyes of the doctor in Zambezi and the consultant in Lusaka, in order to send me down to Salisbury at just that time.

That weekend with my parents was delightful, and on Monday, Dad left us to start a week of a training course he and a colleague were running for many of the senior farmers of the country. He returned to the city on the Tuesday, leaving his colleague to run the course. Dad then began to lead a two-day seminar with all his company's senior people from throughout the whole of southern Africa. The objective was to plan a five-year strategy for all aspects of the business. The day went well and he returned home that evening, but was coughing badly. By 10pm I had called the doctor and Dad was rushed into hospital with pneumonia. About noon the next day he had a massive heart attack and they were unable to resuscitate him. The news of his death had a strong impact on both the groups with whom he was working at the time, many of whom were a similar age to my sixty-one-year-old father. Many of them attended Dad's funeral service, and the church was full and overflowing. It was so encouraging to see the respect in which he was held both by individuals and by the firm for which he worked as technical advisor for the whole of southern Africa.

A loving heavenly Father had made it possible for me to be in Salisbury, not only to support my mother, but to enjoy that special weekend together with both my parents. Then I was able to stay on and help Mum to buy a house more suitable for her living alone, assisting her in the move and settling into the new place, before I finally returned to Zambia six weeks later.

One special joy came when my mother was enabled to visit us at Lukolwe. By then she was seventy and had been suffering from chronic lymphatic leukaemia (CLL) for at least the previous seven years, as well as further health problems. For a time it was a battle for me to agree to her visit as I knew that if she developed an infection while she was with us, she would be unlikely to survive. As I talked with the Lord about it, I began to accept that it was her choice and she was conscious of the consequences. Life, as we lived it, was far more primitive than in the city. Accepting that it might cost her life meant that I was able to hand the burden over to a loving heavenly Father and had real peace.

Mum later described her visit as her trip of a lifetime. We took her on some of our journeys out into the villages for immunisation work, and also a round trip of the greater area around us, staying with a godly Luvale couple who were missionaries to their own people. Mum was amazed at the love and care given by our Luvale friends around us.

Mum did not develop an infection while with us, but the day she flew back home she went down with a severe one and was hospitalised for a time. She still counted it worthwhile!

A couple of years later (1982) I travelled down to Salisbury in order to spend a holiday week or so with my mother. To my surprise, her friend met me at the airport. As we travelled back into town she asked whether I wanted to go to the house first or straight to the hospital. That was the first I knew of something wrong as, while I was travelling, messages had not reached me.

Mum was extremely ill with an infection, had been hospitalised and was not expected to survive. Her condition was bad enough that I called my brother, who came up from South Africa for a few days but had to return to his home, as his wife was booked for major surgery. He left that Easter weekend, not expecting to see Mum again.

Spending all of each day in the hospital I helped nurse Mum, who gradually improved, but appeared to have lost her ability to balance, and her memory had deteriorated badly. After she was discharged from hospital, we did some detective work and realised that some of the drugs she was taking were causing the ataxia and the memory loss. Stopping those errant sleeping pills, now no longer on the market, changed the scene completely and she made a steady recovery.

I cared for her in Salisbury, renamed Harare that year, for six weeks and it was a truly blessed time together, perhaps the best time that I can ever remember with my mother.

Nicki's original short-term visit to Lukolwe meant she was there to share another family crisis. One day in March 1984 the Ferguson family were away, and Nicki and I went to take the two-way radio contact at 12.30pm. A message came for me that my mother had had a stroke the previous night, was in hospital and not expected to live. The message continued that I should try to go down to Harare as soon as possible.

Having completed the radio broadcast, we prayed together and I asked the Lord to take Mum home as soon as possible. She had suffered from CLL for more than ten years and had other serious medical conditions and just longed to go to be with the Lord. My father had died a decade earlier so she lived alone. Radio contact at 5.30pm brought the news that she had taken her last breath at one o'clock.

By that second radio broadcast, Nicki and I had made most of the preparations to leave Lukolwe, and we set off for Chavuma Mission where we spent the night, having crossed the Zambezi River on our home-made pontoon in the dark. Early the next morning we set off cross-country on the 885km journey to Lusaka, another long day of travel over rough roads. We had arranged to stay in the Africa Evangelical Fellowship (AEF) rest home where we were to share a bungalow with others. What a relief it was to me when we arrived to find we were actually sharing accommodation with those dear friends of mine from Chizera Mission, whom I had not seen for some time. It was so good to talk and to know their loving support. They had even prepared a meal for us. Up until that time the pressure of preparations for leaving Lukolwe and the travelling had meant I had scarcely begun to grieve.

The next morning we again set off for the next stage of the 1,600km journey down to Harare. All told, it was a good journey and we had to laugh when we realised that we had arrived before my brother who only had to fly up from Port Elizabeth, South Africa (three hours' flying time). He, too, was relieved when we met him at the airport!

Through all of that time, Nicki's presence was very precious. To have made that journey alone would have been so much harder. Later when working together to pack up the remnants of my mother's life and home before returning to Zambia, her companionship and assistance was invaluable.

We had only been back in Lukolwe for a short time when I contracted an unpleasant chest infection. But life was full and it did not get too much attention. We went out to the Copperbelt for official medical meetings, and then went down to Lusaka to meet Nicki's father, Geoffrey, who was flying out for a long visit. The cough had not responded well to antibiotics, so I was on a second course of them as we met Geoffrey and then drove down to Livingstone and Victoria Falls (500km).

Despite having lived in southern Africa for more than thirty-five years, I had only paid an overnight, brief visit to Victoria Falls on one occasion, so it was an exciting time for all of us. Geoffrey's photographic tripod became a useful walking stick as I kept active despite feeling weak. From there we introduced Geoffrey to cross-country travel Zambian-style as we drove from Lusaka back to Lukolwe, via back roads and the Kafue game park. His visit was a time of hard work but, as with my own mother, a very special time for him as he experienced life spent with the people in our isolated community.

Meanwhile, I was still not very well and growing weaker, although Geoffrey had no idea of this. He left us one day, and the following day Nicki and I went over to Chavuma to see the resident mission doctor. He was shocked when he was given the initial blood test results and went and rechecked them for himself, as my white cell count was exceedingly low. I can remember him viewing the chest X-ray with horror and saying in surprise, 'You've got pneumonia.'

The outcome of this was that a few days later I was flown out in an AEF mission Cessna plane on the first stage of the long journey to Cape Town for medical treatment. What a blessing it was to have Nicki with me through all that difficult journey and for the first few weeks in Cape Town, which included major surgery. The journey from Lukolwe involved four two-hour flights, starting in a small Cessna and finishing in a jumbo jet! Nicki flew back to London from there in order to be her friend's bridesmaid, having extended her visit from six to nine months.

It was not known at that time whether I could ever return to Lukolwe, although I believed that it would happen. The initial response of the consultants had been that I should not return, but, despite the surgery, my immune system began to function somewhat better. One Sunday the Christian consultant (a friend), invited us to his home for a meal. He then shared that he believed God had shown him that it was indeed right for me to return to Lukolwe, and three months after arriving in Cape Town I was allowed to return to Zambia. Interestingly, it took another almost thirty years before the chronic immune deficiency was correctly diagnosed and treated.

Sometimes we can make a decision, such as not accepting another short-term worker, and God turns it around. He sent Nicki to be the support I needed during that very difficult year and I was so grateful.

For several years I used the book *Streams in the Desert* that Susie had given me, then left it in my parents' home when I went to Zambia. Many years later I found it on my mother's bedside after she had died. It was easy to see what comfort and challenge she had found there, as the book is marked throughout with her notes. It showed too the cost to parents whose children serve God in many isolated or distant parts of the world, and also revealed to me how much she had prayed for me. It is still brings back treasured memories.

I did not have a husband and children to increase the pain my mother bore as a result of my being so far away, as is the case for many missionary families. But during the later years of her life she would dearly have liked me to be able to be the support she often needed, particularly during the ten years after Dad died and she lived with leukaemia. Yet, as told above, it was often made possible for me to be there at times of crisis.

Postal system

By the time I went to Lukolwe, I was quite accustomed to seeing snakes, but they never lost their threat. We needed to be aware and be careful. Patients were seldom brought into the hospital with snake bites, as the venom too often resulted in death before they could reach us. The black mamba was one of the most dangerous and its venom could kill an adult within twenty minutes. We had various experiences with snakes of all sizes, from small puff adders to ten-foot-long black mambas. The main type of cobra in our area could spit venom with amazing accuracy over a distance of up to ten feet. It usually aimed for the eyes, thus immobilising its prey. Untreated, such an attack could cause blindness.

On one occasion I had been across the Zambezi River and collected a missionary schoolteacher who had come for a visit. Such a trip involved stopping at the post office and collecting our huge duffel bag of mail, then, when back at Lukolwe, sorting it and delivering the contents to the various folk. Post arrived intermittently, whenever we had a trip across the river to collect it, and the postal system in that isolated area was erratic at best. Six weeks from posting a letter to a reply was speedy. Christmas cards were not uncommonly delivered as late as July of the following year!

That day I had shown my visitor her room and she was settling down for a rest. Having sorted all the incoming letters, it took two arms to carry the pile to be taken to the Fergusons' house. Exiting my back door I felt something catch around my ankles, but the load I was carrying prevented my actually seeing what it was. Presuming some of the bark rope used to tie up the firewood we used for cooking and boiling water had been carelessly left lying around as a trip hazard, I felt mildly irritated. Peering around the load you may imagine my horror at seeing a large cobra twisted around both ankles! Thankfully, the snake had as much of a fright as I did and went one way while I went the other. It had already bitten a hen in a cage near my back door. The hen died, but that probably contributed to the fact that I was not bitten, and I was too close to have venom shot into my eyes. The snake tried to hide in a drain, which gave me time to shout for help, and it paid the price for being so dangerously close to the house.

Interestingly, even years later after I was back in the UK, I still reacted negatively to anything (perhaps just grass) brushing across my ankles, or stepped very warily when the trees had dropped their leaves into heaps on the steps outside. Snakes loved to hide under fallen leaves to keep warm.

Immunisation campaign

Although we had been immunising children at the health centre as much as possible, it was inconsistent and erratic. During my first five years, there had been epidemics of whooping cough and measles.

In the early years during the first whooping cough epidemic I experienced, there were around 200 adults and children resident in our tiny hospital. People were everywhere, in the wards, the open thatched kitchens and anywhere else they could find to lay their sleeping mats. At another time the picture was similar, this time owing to an outbreak of measles. During such epidemics the high mortality and morbidity were unacceptable, but in the villages even more children and adults died. Many children who survived were left with damaged eyes or even blindness, loss of hearing or, for some, brain damage. Many became severely malnourished, with resulting loss of resistance to other infections. For us, the workload was enormous, and I look back with much thanksgiving for the staff, who had little training but worked so hard. Even I went down with whooping cough, which was most unpleasant.

We began an immunisation campaign in 1975. The Zambian government, encouraged by the World Health Organization (WHO), were making an effort to try to fully immunise all children in Zambia, aged fourteen and under. They supplied the vaccines, but the logistics of transporting them so they remained viable was ours, and took considerable planning. I even bought a small refrigerator that would sit in the back of my Land Cruiser and run off the car battery when we were travelling to collect vaccines, or when we went on trips to the village. When stationary, the refrigerator ran off a paraffin burner.

Vaccines all have differing schedules of administration, differing times between each dose, and differing shelf life. This challenged us and it took considerable research to learn the parameters, and to use them effectively. We might see one child and give a triple vaccine (diphtheria/whooping cough/tetanus, known as DPT), then for the second dose the child might be, perhaps, in another village area, but receive their second dose in reasonable time. Months might pass and they not be seen again for almost a year. Knowing the parameters would mean we could still give the child their third dose and know it would be reasonably effective, even though the ideal would have been for them to receive each dose a month apart. More than a year's duration for the third dose meant starting again from the beginning, and so on. For some of the vaccines, heat or sunlight would destroy them. There was no visual indication which vaccines had lost their potency, so we had to maintain a strict regime as far as possible.

With this in control, we started to register every child within a 1,500-square-mile area. A number had received some of the vaccines when attending the hospital with their mother. For a long time before this, we had used their outpatient visits, as far as possible, to immunise the children before anyone received medical care. But that was not enough, so we visited the headman of each village in the area, some very isolated, and explained the effects of vaccines and why we wanted to register every child. They cooperated very well and, later on, helped with the campaign by a rivalry between each village area in the effort to achieve the goal of full immunisation for every child.

The plan was to try to weigh each child monthly, and to immunise each one against DPT, polio and later, measles, when that vaccine was developed and became available. Smallpox vaccine was given to all children and adults. Looking back, it is quite encouraging to realise we were part of the campaign to eliminate smallpox.

One of the issues that challenged us came from the cultural habit of sending children off to live for months at a time with their grandparents or other family members in distant villages. Of course, it was seldom a priority to send their immunisation card with the child! So we might meet them anywhere on our travels and the distances were vast. I soon learned to make and take our own register of all the children and their vaccine records whenever we went out to any village area. To add to this confusion, most children had several names. If born in a hospital they probably had an English-sounding name, but the parents would usually use their African name and the grandmothers would each have given the child a different name, which they would use. Which name did we register them under? What happened when the child was with their grandmother and using that name? A 'surname' was a concept not previously considered. How does one build in a consistency so that other people would know which child we were seeking? Gradually we learned to cope reasonably well with these and other challenges.

The whole campaign was maintained over the last fifteen years I was at Lukolwe and for at least a few years afterwards, while Nicki was still there. It was hard work (sometimes exhaustingly so), challenging and yet so worthwhile. On each trip to the villages a few of the Christians travelled with us and gossiped the gospel. One dear lady became a close friend as we made so many journeys together. During the monthly overnight stays she designated herself our cook and bottle washer and was so caring and helpful.

But it was ten years after the campaign started before any local person indicated they appreciated that vaccinations were of value. One day an older mother walked about thirty miles in to the health centre. She carried her baby on her back and had twins of just under four walking beside her. She also carried their food, blankets and a mat in a huge basin on her head. Surprised to see her, I asked why she had come in, expecting that one of them was ill. Her reply was to say that she had brought her baby in for his measles jab, as there was an outbreak of measles across the plain from where they lived and he hadn't yet had the vaccine. Then I asked why she had walked so far when we were scheduled to travel to her village the next day. Her reply was that the trip might have been delayed (not too unusual if there was a mother in complicated labour or other medical emergency), then went on to say that the reason she thought the vaccine was important was 'because it works, of course'! What a glorious statement and a real encouragement to us. We had worked so hard and long, often in the face of minimal understanding, and needed that boost! We gave them a lift home the following day as we went out for the clinics.

Every child was vaccinated up to, and sometimes past, the WHO targets for herd immunity. Then the epidemic of measles that instigated Olive's trip to the health centre surrounded our area of protection. Throughout non-vaccinated areas, measles was just as virulent as it had been previously. As far as we could ascertain, not one child we had vaccinated developed severe measles, although a few who were heavily exposed to the disease did have an attenuated attack with no resulting long-term debility. After commencing the immunisation campaign, we never again had the health centre full of desperately ill children and adults as a result of such an epidemic. Occasionally we would have children brought in from distant areas where they had had no help, and they would be as ill as those we had seen in earlier years.

Interestingly, it became more difficult to reach and immunise the second generation of children born to already immunised mothers. Those young women had never seen the severity of outbreaks of measles, whooping cough or polio, and so felt resistant to their babies being given injections that often resulted in a wakeful night afterwards. The measles epidemic mentioned above was the catalyst to bring them flocking back to have their babies immunised. It also reminded the grandparents of the severity of those soon-forgotten illnesses.

Later I was encouraged by a government official that our area had among the highest immunisation rate throughout Zambia. It felt good after the effort we had put into the campaign. But the biggest reward was to see the improvement in health among the children, and the reduction of the incidence of those terrible, debilitating diseases.

The bilharzia project

During the early 1980s, with many schoolchildren underweight and not growing well, we decided that as so many suffered from an infestation of the parasite bilharzia (schistosomiasis mansoni), we needed to do something about it. After considerable planning, we started a project to check every single schoolchild in the primary schools around the health centre. This meant checking their stool (faeces) specimens under the microscope for hookworm and bilharzia. Shockingly, but not unexpectedly, we found that 100 per cent of the children had hookworm eggs and 97 per cent showed bilharzia eggs.

This started a dilemma because it was rather difficult to obtain the drugs needed to treat them, particularly in the quantities we now realised we needed. The treatment for hookworm was fairly inexpensive, but the treatment (praziquantel) for bilharzia was very costly, although easy to administer. Then a group of people from Kitwe on the Zambian Copperbelt decided that they would try to sponsor us. They used various ways of earning funds and even held a concert performance in one of the cinemas. By this means they brought in enough for us to buy the praziquantel, with sufficient to treat every single local schoolchild.

We had not only examined every child's stool for the parasites, but over a period of many years, we had already routinely weighed all children from birth to age fifteen and recorded their slow level of growth. The vast majority were in the range classed as moderately to severely malnourished. In addition, the teachers felt that many children were too sleepy in school to work effectively.

We continued regularly weighing every child in each school and we treated them for hookworm and bilharzia. With our small staff this was a real effort, but we felt that it was worthwhile. There were other schools we visited, too far away for the children to be tested and treated, although being within our immunisation campaign area they were regularly weighed and immunised. They worked as a control for the ones we did treat.

Over the next two years we followed up these children, retesting them and finding that the vast majority were completely free of hookworm and bilharzia, although they would almost certainly have been exposed to the parasites again. Those that still showed eggs in their stools were retreated. As we weighed them regularly it was interesting to note that the treated children all gained weight at a more rapid rate than those in the control schools. Most of them moved out of the range of malnutrition into that of healthy children, although their diet was unchanged. The teachers in the various local schools (where they had been treated) stated that the children were coming in to school much more alert. They were remaining alert through the school day and so they were actually able to learn more. Sadly this was anecdotal, as there were no set exams and no other ways of testing educational changes, so the teachers' thoughts on these matters had to be taken as they were given.

Definitely those children were healthier and gained weight and it was interesting to see that they continued to progress steadily. Over the next few years they seemed to grow and mature more quickly than the untreated children in the control school areas. In addition, repeated testing showed that few of them became heavily reinfested with either parasite.

It is a real tribute to the staff of our rural health centre that they were willing to give of themselves in order to make this campaign effective. There were no trained laboratory staff or pharmacists. I had taught our locally trained Dressers to use a microscope and do various laboratory tests for parasites, including malaria. They managed to maintain their usual workload, operated the single microscope to make the necessary tests, administered the medications, etc. It was hard work for all of us, but very rewarding.

Was it only one day?

Not long ago, rereading some Bible notes from 1985, I came across a sentence that challenged me:

> God has a marvellous and brilliant way of camouflaging opportunities to look like difficulties.[13]

This reminded me of a day in about 1982 when God taught me a wonderful lesson. At the time I did not know this quotation and could not see any of the opportunities! Rereading my journal from that day reminded me vividly of the story.

It all happened in one day – and the lesson started very early! In some ways it was a very ordinary day. Daily life in the African bush was filled with challenges. But it was also a day when God taught me a lesson about how our attitudes affect our responses to situations, particularly our negative attitudes.

---

[13] Selwyn Hughes and Trevor J Partridge, *Through the Bible Every Day in One Year*, 22nd January (Farnham: CWR, 1985).

As usual I woke at 5am, listened to the news on the radio for five minutes and had a cup of coffee before spending time reading God's Word. A busy day lay ahead and I had been up in the night for the birth of a healthy little baby. Breakfast followed and then I went and collected the small pickup vehicle ready for when the workmen arrived at 7am.

The first job of the day was to collect a load of thick blocks of soil and roots (sods) and take them behind the hospital for completing the pit latrines. The day before, workmen had dug the sods out from a small plain down near our local river. Two of the workmen loaded up the pickup and as I tried to drive it off, it sank up to the axles in the soft soil. One look and we all knew that it would not come out easily, so the men began to remove the load again and meanwhile I climbed back up the hill to my house to collect a shovel with which to dig out the wheels.

I can remember so clearly taking that spade in my hand and feeling under a great deal of pressure over the work needing to be done. Patients and staff needed me at the hospital. I stopped and thought of the desperate cry that was in my heart as I walked up the hill. 'Why? It seems so hard.' Standing the spade against the wall I went into the house, knelt by my bed and asked God that question.

It seemed as though a voice spoke to me: 'Read Philippians 4:4.'

'Yes, Lord, I know that it says "Rejoice always", but I can't. It is too hard.'

'Read Philippians 4:4.'

'I want to obey You, but ...'

'Read Philippians 4:4.'

So I finally reached out and took my Bible and opened it at Philippians 4:4

What does it say? As I read it I felt ashamed.

> Rejoice *in the Lord* always: and again I say, Rejoice.
> (Philippians 4:4, KJV, my emphasis)

As I looked at those words the whole picture changed. Wow, I could do that! I could rejoice in God Himself, in His Son who saved me, in His Spirit who gives me life – the One who loves me and cares even when things are hard. It was a joy to say, 'Yes, Lord, I can rejoice in You and what You have done, even when other things are tough,' and hand over the whole situation to Him. I walked down that hill carrying the spade and singing with joy.

Now, you would expect things to improve, but my lesson for the day was not over! Yet my attitude to it had changed completely.

We dug the little pickup out, reloaded it and it promptly sank again to the axles! Then I had to ask for help. Lorne Ferguson was busy preparing for another Bible teaching camp so I had not wanted to bother him. When called, he willingly put aside his Bible to take his big four-wheel drive truck down near the river to pull us out – and immediately sank to the axles in that vehicle too. Finally, after first winching his own truck out, then attaching the winch to our pickup, he pulled us out and I drove to the area behind the hospital with the needed sods. What a relief!

Of course the work in the hospital had started at 7am too, so by that time I was late and needed to make a round of all the inpatients, discuss with the staff and prepare the stock medicines from the pharmacy. I was still able to rejoice in the Lord, but not the circumstances, which were very pressured.

By 8.30am there was our regular two-way radio contact with the other mission stations around, and Betty Lou Ferguson usually handled that. A short time later, she arrived at the examination room door with a message she had received telling me I had to go down immediately to Zambezi Township to collect some day-old chickens that had been flown in from Lusaka the day before. The chickens had been ordered to improve our food supply with eggs and meat, and needed to be transported during the first twenty-four hours of life. Zambezi Township was across the Zambezi River (no bridges) and a very hard and tiring drive.

My response to Betty Lou, who had known nothing of the challenges of the day thus far, was to just burst into tears. It was too much!

But there seemed no alternative. Calming down and remembering that God was there, I prepared my Toyota Land Cruiser and set off on the journey of about sixty miles each way. The first part took me past the home of a lovely elderly Christian man, Sambaza, and I called in to tell him where I was going, asking him to pray. Instead he announced that he would travel with me across the Zambezi River as far as Chavuma Mission, spend time with friends and return with me later that day. The company was welcome and we had a good time of fellowship together.

About seven miles and nearly an hour of driving from Lukolwe, we passed through a village and, as we left it, several men ran out and waved the vehicle down. They had a woman who had stayed in the village to have her baby. The baby was born safely sometime during the night, but the placenta had not came out. The woman was bleeding heavily and would probably have died if she had remained in the village. Resignedly, I told them to bring her and I would take them to Chavuma Mission. Sometimes it was discouraging to realise that mothers would still stay in the villages for the birth of their babies, despite the dangers. In addition, such stops could be time-consuming indeed – they initially explained the problem (whatever it might be), prepared the patient, food, blankets, and finally loaded her and the rest of the family into the vehicle.

With the mother, the baby and a whole crowd of family filling the rear section, we set off again for the last three miles to the river. One and a half hours after leaving Lukolwe, we arrived at the river crossing to be met with a shout from the distant bank telling us that the pontoon (ferry) was out of action. There would be no crossing there that day. I put my head on the steering wheel and wept again!

Sambaza, my friend (who was about ninety-two at that time), decided to go across the river in the dugout canoe. I had no choice but to turn around and go home again, this time including the patient with serious maternity complications. She was too ill to be put into the canoe and then to have to walk up Chavuma hill to the hospital. Before he left, Sambaza prayed with me and I set off back on the track that led home to Lukolwe.

Once there it was possible to save the patient's life by removing the placenta and leave mother and baby safe. After a bite to eat and a top-up with fuel for the Toyota, I set out again, well after midday, to try to reach Zambezi Township. The first twenty miles to and from the Zambezi River crossing had taken about three and a half hours back to the starting point, then the time spent caring for the maternity patient. Now there was the full journey ahead down the far more precarious track winding its way south on our west side of the Zambezi River. Two of the workmen accompanied me for the help that would be needed, particularly over the primitive bridge structures built across streams and for the ferry crossing.

It took more than three hours to go the thirty miles to reach the Catholic Mission south of us. Then we pulled ourselves by hand across the river on their ferry that was hung from a cable. There was real relief in finally reaching Zambezi Township by dusk. The chickens would just have to survive for another night there, although hungry! After finding a safe place for them at a local farm institute, I begged a bed from my Indian friends. Early the next morning we loaded up the Toyota with forty-four-gallon drums of fuel and the boxes of baby chickens and made our way back, crossing the Zambezi River again on the same ferry, arriving home mid-afternoon.

That day is still so clear in my mind, not for the pain endured, but for the lesson God taught me about my attitude to difficulties. From the moment I knelt by that bed and handed it all back to Him, realising that I could rejoice in Him at all times, there had been a deep peace and a joy within that the drama of the day did not dull. It was hard, I was exhausted, there had been tears more than once, but God knew all about it and was there with me.

> God has a marvellous and brilliant way of camouflaging opportunities to look like difficulties …
> We must be careful not to interpret the days of obscurity and isolation as meaningless and unimportant. It is there that God prepares His servants for the spiritual challenges that lie ahead.[14]

[14] Selwyn Hughes and Trevor J. Partridge, Philippians 1:6, *Through the Bible Every Day in One Year*, 22nd and 23rd January (Farnham: CWR, 1985). Used with permission.

Some of our more memorable patients

The medical work was routine in many ways, with the most common diseases being malaria, diarrhoea and chest infections. The daily flow of people with aches and pains, burns, maternity, childcare and general problems kept us busy. But from time to time the more unusual situations brought unexpected challenges.

When patients needed more medical care than we could give, most of the time it was possible, if not easy, to make the decision and know that we could transport them across the Zambezi River. But there were times when that river crossing was literally impossible.

One night in the late 1960s we had a woman in labour. I had not been at Lukolwe very long so was still learning what was, and was not, possible. She came in from a nearby village with unexpected complications and I felt helpless and completely out of my depth. I made the decision that it would be right to try to make a potentially difficult night-time crossing of the river to transport her to a doctor who could operate and save mother and baby. A colleague graciously accepted my decision and we loaded up his vehicle with the patient and her relatives and set off for the river, arriving there shortly after 10pm.

Once we reached the riverbank it was obvious that there was no way of taking a vehicle across the flooded river that night. The family were prepared to try to use the government 'banana boat' (similar to a large dugout canoe, but made of fibreglass), and walk up to Chavuma Mission on the far bank. But there was one problem. When we arrived we found the boat had a fist-sized hole in the base. This was stuffed with rags, but each time they pushed away from the bank the water pressure forced the rags out of the hole and the boat flooded.

After a number of attempts, and considerable dismay on my part, we all accepted that it was impossible to cross that night. Everyone was loaded back into the vehicle and we returned to Lukolwe. By then it was well after midnight. Thankfully, after a very difficult labour, calling on resources I did not know I had, we were able to save the life of the mother, although not the baby. This experience taught me some of the parameters by which we had to live!

Chilombo

One day a young child was brought into our clinic from her village twenty-five miles away. Her mother was hoping we could help her, but was also very fatalistic. The spirits had planned it, therefore Chilombo obviously was to become one of those useless children who crawl around the ground all their lives. The tiny girl was either born with a shortened Achilles tendon or, most likely, had had polio in the first year of her life, leaving her with a thin weak leg and a foot extended in such a way that she would never be able to walk on it.

She was brought in to us when she was about two. It was one of the rare occasions when a missionary doctor was visiting. He examined the extended foot and offered to operate and correct the deformity. But the trouble was that it would mean the family had to travel 100 miles down to the nearest mission hospital with the doctor, and the resulting cost to them all seemed too great. They went home and worked in their fields. They told me the spirits had ordained their child would be deformed and it was pointless to fight that fact. They had already been to the witchdoctor and he could do nothing, although that would have cost them dearly.

For the people of the area, the actual cost of such a journey down to the distant hospital would not just be financial. Families would go together, not knowing the duration of their stay. Back home, who would cultivate their crops, their only food source for the coming year? Where would they find money to buy food to feed the family while away? If they had any livestock, selling it to cover costs was impoverishing long-term. If they could borrow the money, how would they pay it back? Daily life was not easy and such a disruption extremely hard.

Chilombo continued to grow, and to crawl around. Her mother became pregnant again and during the pregnancy they all had increasing contact with us and trust began to grow. Then the mother found a patch of pale skin on her own face and was anxious in case it might be leprosy. The whole family, including Chilombo, quickly accepted a lift down to Chitokoloki Hospital, 100 miles away, for the mother to be seen by the doctor. Once there, at my suggestion, the mission doctor delayed examining the mother until he had operated on Chilombo's leg, putting it into a plaster-of-Paris cast. Their new baby girl was born safely, and then he examined the pale skin on the mother's face and confirmed that she did not have leprosy. The family returned to us, the mission health centre nearest their home, and with the help of a stick, Chilombo began to stand on the leg encased in plaster. For her that was a day of real triumph as she looked down at her baby sister and said, 'See, I'm bigger than you. I can stand!'

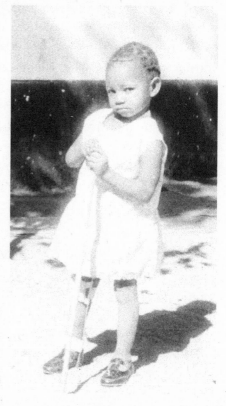

Being the one who arranged all of this and giving a great deal of time to the family over a period of years, Chilombo became a special little girl to me. Besides engineering the surgery, caring for Chilombo while in the plaster of Paris, removing it and doing physiotherapy, I was able to find suitable shoes in a box of used clothing and make a Heath Robinson calliper for the leg from strong wire, with several more as she grew bigger. Throughout it all, her mother's lack of motivation had to be battled constantly!

Chilombo will always limp and have a leg that is weaker and thinner than usual. But after recovery from the surgery she soon discarded the home-made support for her leg and began to walk unaided. By the time she was old enough to go to school she was able to walk the six miles either way every day, and to take her part as a productive member of the community.

Her parents acknowledged that in some things the God of the missionaries was more powerful than the spirits who surrounded them each day. Their friendly relationship with us continued through the years and they often heard the good news of God's unfailing love, but continued to live in fear and bondage to those same spirits.

The last time I saw Chilombo, aged about sixteen, she was a real joy to behold and living a fulfilled and normal life despite her limp.

The dangers of being prepared . . .

Many years later, we had a middle-aged man pushed in on a bicycle from a distant village, arriving late one evening. As was the custom, and in readiness for anything he might encounter, he had been carrying his home-made lightweight, but sharp, axe, hooked over his shoulder. This had slipped and cut through the back of his lower leg. His Achilles tendon was severed, except for a paper-thin section about a centimetre wide. It was amazing that it still held together as, if it had broken completely, the ends would have retracted way up into the leg muscles. What I had learned during training days told me that it was a very serious problem and could potentially leave the man crippled for life. The danger of that paper-thin connection breaking was immense.

It was one of those occasions when there was absolutely no possibility of transporting him to a doctor. The only option was to operate to try to save the situation, but I had never done anything like that before. After suturing the tendon back together and closing the wound, the leg was immobilised in a plaster-of-Paris cast. He was soon using a pair of crutches to allow healing. To our amazement, a year later he could walk with scarcely a limp. At times like that, when way out of my comfort zone, many arrow prayers shot up to a heavenly Father.

Meningitis

One evening a child of about three years old was brought into the health centre. He was very ill, had been carried a long distance and his life was in the balance. Diagnosing meningitis, I spent most of the night caring for him and he began to improve by about 5am, so I went off for an hour of sleep before the start of a new day. When I returned to the hospital, the child had gone. He had been taken off to a local village. For me it was one of those deeply discouraging times, being very tired and having literally worked all night to try to save him.

We continued to pray for the boy and that the high doses of penicillin he had received would be sufficient to save his life. Later we learned that one of the local witchdoctors had heard about his illness – news spreads fast in that environment. The witchdoctor had sent men to the health centre to tell the parents that the *chindele* (white man's) medicines would not work for such an illness and the only hope was to take the boy to him for treatment in the nearby village. We heard them drumming over the child throughout the next two days and nights. Can you imagine that poor child's pain, with a headache and all that drumming right beside him? When he recovered, of course, the witchdoctor took all the credit.

An interesting aspect, learned later, was that the witchdoctor himself had not been willing to step into the mission health centre, believing his powers would not work there.

Bewitched?

One day while at home with another young nurse, who had come out on a short-term visit, there was a loud clapping outside. One of our staff was calling us to come quickly because a child was bewitched. Even from the house we could hear the screaming. The two-year-old child, with a relatively minor illness, was in a cot at the end of the ward. He and his mother were the only people in evidence. The child's high-pitched screaming was such as I had never previously heard and he was inconsolable. All the other patients and relatives had fled as far away as possible. They were all convinced he was bewitched.

We went to him, and were unsure of what to do. We knew of evil spirits being cast out of people by the power of God, but had never experienced anything like this. Even our staff had fled. It was nerve-rackingly scary. Eventually I prayed that if it was the power of evil at work, then God would overcome it and heal the child. It was a simple prayer voiced out loud, and to our amazement, the child immediately quietened and reached for his mother. The staff, patients and relatives all gasped aloud from outside, where they had been peering through the glassless windows, and it was the talk of the day that the missionaries' God had greater powers than the evil spirits.

The child recovered fully from his minor illness, and the parents went home marvelling. That was the only time we faced this type of problem in the health centre, and it was indeed terrifying.

Agony

On another occasion a very elderly man was brought in to us. He had been brought in by his friends, hanging in a blanket from a pole carried on their shoulders. They had travelled about sixty miles and taken three days to reach us. The patient was in a very poor condition and suffering from acute retention of urine as the result of an enlarged prostate, so we treated him with antibiotics and an intravenous drip. Of course, a catheter brought immediate relief.

But he needed more medical help than we could give. Leaving the catheter in place we loaded him into the Toyota Land Cruiser and drove the six-hour journey across the Zambezi River and down to the nearest government hospital. There, to my amazement, the resident government doctor did absolutely nothing, except to keep him in for a few days. He then sent the patient back to us on the bus and on foot, with the same grubby catheter still in place.

After a short time with us, we again set off for a hospital. This time we took him to Chitokoloki, our nearest mission hospital. There they took good care of him, operated on his enlarged prostate and finally brought him back to us. That little old wizened man then set off on foot for the sixty-mile journey home, having expressed his gratitude to us for saving his life.

That should have been the last we saw of him but, one day many months later, I heard a clap outside the door and answered it. There stood the same man with his granddaughter, maybe ten years old. He had insisted on carrying a scrawny chicken on his back like a baby, while his granddaughter had carried a huge basin of cassava meal. They had walked the sixty miles from their home to express their thanks with these gifts of food. It was a humbling moment.

And there was more to the story. For the first and probably the only time in my years at Lukolwe, that day I had no food to prepare for my main meal. It was provided through that gift. How grateful I was.

Emergency surgery

Late one afternoon a young girl of about twelve years old was brought to us from a nearby village. She had acute abdominal pain and was in agony. Immediately I examined her I realised she needed surgery urgently. It was already about 5.30pm and the Zambezi River, some one to two hours' travel time from us, was not crossable in the dark after about 6pm. We prayed and then loaded up the Toyota Land Cruiser with fuel, paddles for the river crossing, the patient and all her family with their bedding, including food for an unknown duration, and set off towards the river. Thankfully, not only was the government ferry working, but also the men were willing to return from their homes and take us across the river, despite the darkness.

The journey down to Zambezi Township and the nearest doctor took another three hours over very rough roads. The child did not complain for the whole journey, but must have been in tremendous pain. There was a different doctor that time and he operated immediately.

We spent the night in a friend's home. Next day we looked in on the recovering patient, collected two forty-four-gallon drums of fuel awaiting transport back to Lukolwe, and set off for home. The men who loaded those heavy drums onto my vehicle refused payment for the work, saying they were 'happy to help because you helped us'. By that stage I was well known in the area, and had a reputation for caring. It was rather special to receive thanks in this way from local people. News, by

153

word of mouth, spreads very fast in such communities, so they would have known about the patient who had arrived the day before. Once again the seemingly impossible was made possible and we were enabled to help save her life.

Ectopic pregnancy

Early one December a middle-aged lady was brought in from a nearby village with severe abdominal pain. Examining her, we could clearly see it was a crisis situation, and she was bleeding internally. We prepared to evacuate her down to the nearest doctor in Zambezi Township. It took time to start two intravenous drips running into her arms and set her up in the 'ambulance' – my Toyota Land Cruiser. With the drip bags tied to the top of the canopy with bandages, the stretcher in the centre and her family crowded all around her in the back of the pickup, we set off for the flooded Zambezi River crossing ten miles away. Having crossed safely on our pontoon (oh, how simple that makes it sound!), we called at Chavuma Mission to check on the patient. There we drained some of the blood from her abdomen into an intravenous bag and poured it back into her veins as we continued the journey down to the doctor. Despite the five hours of travelling and the very rough roads in a heavy, uncomfortable, bouncing vehicle she arrived at the hospital safely and went straight into emergency life-saving surgery.

Later in the month she returned to her village, having been warned not to become pregnant again for several months. Thus it was, when she came back in to us before the middle of the following January complaining of abdominal pain again, she adamantly denied that there was any possibility she could be pregnant. It took considerable time to elicit the truth. Rather mystified by her serious symptoms, we again set off for Zambezi Township under emergency conditions. Once again she arrived in time for immediate surgery for a second ectopic pregnancy, and her life was saved.

That was the only time that two such emergency trips had to be made for one patient within six weeks, and this stretched us to the limit both in diagnostic skills and the sheer physical challenges of preparing and making those trips to the government hospital. Of course, back at base the work just waited until we returned!

Forgiveness

One day each week we went out to immunise children in different village areas between twenty and thirty miles away. Once a month, when the moon was brightest and thus giving us light all evening, we went from Friday to Sunday, doing a large clinic near the school in Sefu on the Friday. There we spent the day weighing and immunising the children, examining any pregnant ladies and attending to others who needed medical care. Then we travelled on to a place called Mukelangombe across a dry flood plain. Somewhere between the two areas we would stop to collect some firewood for cooking purposes.

At Mukelangombe we had a second full day's clinic on the Saturday. Usually I was responsible for the vehicle preparation, the driving, preparing, giving and recording the vaccines, etc. One of the hospital Dressers would be there to weigh the children. As mentioned earlier, often some of the local Christians would join us and they , particularly the women, sat around among the families chatting the gospel. One of the ladies, Nyakayinda, became a real friend. She would go along to prepare our food during the days away, as her service to us and to the Lord.

As my workload was quite high on such trips, both in preparation, driving over the poor tracks (where ten miles per hour was too fast), then taking a considerable amount of the medical responsibility, it was discussed and decided that any Christians going with us could not be collected from their home villages, but had to bring themselves in to the hospital in time to leave early in the morning. This was the norm for church services and hospital visits, so not asking too much. As far as we knew, everyone involved was happy with this arrangement.

One day, just before leaving the house to go to the hospital, I was startled to find a church and village elder at my door. He had walked in three miles to arrive before 7am. That was unusual!

He had come to complain that he was not being given the respect that was due to him as an elder. In particular his complaint was that he was not being collected from his village before, and returned there after, a trip out to immunise children. He proceeded to accuse me of racism, stating that if he had a white skin then I would have fetched him from his village and taken him home after each trip. His attitude shocked me to the core that morning and, when I understood what he was saying, I responded quietly but clearly, *'Munanguvangila'* ('You are making a false accusation'). This was a powerful statement in Luvale. He was obviously shaken by it and quietly left to return to his home.

But feeling deep pain at his words and accusations, I went and knelt by my bed to talk it over with the Lord before going to work at the hospital. If there was truth in what he said, I needed to understand it. If not, to forgive him. Kneeling there that morning it was possible to, as it were, hold the accusation and pain out to the Lord with open hands and ask God to make my forgiveness real. I rose to face the day with a deep peace of heart despite the sadness, and made a choice that whenever the conversation came to mind I would not entertain it or discuss it with others. It had been handed over to my heavenly Father.

A year later, something happened that made me realise that God had not only enabled me to forgive the man, but to forget it too. A group of the church elders came for a visit and to talk over their view of the medical work and how I was living day by day. This was not unusual and was a helpful form of accountability. Of course, the whole discussion was all in the Luvale language.

We had a good time together and they were very encouraging. Then just when I thought we had finished, the senior man, Sambaza, asked me, 'What about your problem with this man?', indicating the elder who had come to my door a year earlier. I was totally blank and in good Luvale fashion asked their forgiveness for not knowing what issue was being mentioned and for them please to elaborate. When reminded of the situation, they then asked me why I had not gone to the elders to have the issue 'judged' by them (an action taken by the elders of the church ostensibly to enable Christians to sort out their issues without having to go to the tribunal courts). My reply was that I had taken it to the Lord, had forgiven

Njimu and left it there. They then asked why I had not told him he was forgiven. When I replied that he had never asked for forgiveness there was quite a silence, then we looked at a few scriptures relating to the subject. The outcome was that very proud man actually apologised to me publicly in front of the other elders.

In addition we had all learned lessons from the incident. God can enable us to forgive and forget. It is not necessary for someone to ask for forgiveness before we can choose to forgive them and, perhaps even more, the lack of humility needed to confess we are wrong can destroy our peace. I had been enabled to genuinely put the incident behind me and had, when challenged, shown I had forgotten about it. But Njimu himself had had no peace and was still struggling with it a year later!

False accusations

One Sunday in 2014 we had some Bible teaching based on Nehemiah 6. It was a challenge as to the way Nehemiah handled persecution, slander and outright lies, putting the work to which he believed God had directed him first and foremost. He just kept on with the job and did not allow opposition to weaken or divert him.

This brought back memories of a time when I felt challenged in that way. For a number of years there had been differences among the missionaries of the wider area with regard to the teaching given by my colleague at Lukolwe. He was accused of non-biblical and even heretical teaching, but in truth I do not believe he was guilty of either. I heard a great deal of what he taught the local people in the Bible camp teaching ministry and had spent much time searching the Scriptures for myself. I believe the actual issues involved often stemmed from differences of opinion and about the attitudes and relationships we, as missionaries, had with the local community.

As a result, and because I was based in the same place as he and his family, my single friends on local mission stations had been told that they were not to entertain me, or have me stay the night as their guest. It was not an easy time, particularly as the expatriates in the area were few and distances great, so we all needed one another. One or two of the single ladies refused to accept this prohibition, and indicated that I was welcome to stay with them, but they suffered as a result too.

One particular evening a pregnant woman in labour developed complications necessitating a caesarean section. This meant taking her to the Zambezi River and making our way across the river on the home-made pontoon, then driving on to the nearest hospital. Thankfully we had heard that a visiting missionary doctor was at Chavuma overnight so that stage of our journey was only a very few miles, but the whole trip took about two hours.

We arrived safely with the distressed mother and her family, and very quickly the caesarean section was performed in the hospital theatre. After mother and baby were transferred to a bed in the ward, we cleared up and cleaned the operating theatre. When the others had left, the visiting doctor asked me to stay behind for a few minutes, and there, talking across the theatre table he said many things I had never expected to hear.

Firstly he told me that I was wrong still to be at Lukolwe because of the 'heretical Bible teacher' who was there with his family. Then he went on to expand on the issue with many words, some very hard to hear, and finally stated that he had recently been in Harare, Zimbabwe (formerly Rhodesia), with the elders from one of the churches that had commended me to the work at

Lukolwe. Seemingly they had told him they did not agree with my remaining at Lukolwe and had already told me so. This was particularly relevant and threatening as several months earlier I had had a letter from them asking about the major issues regarding division that he was raising. Having replied to those elders and also sent copies to the leaders of my other three supporting churches, I had not yet heard from them. (Such delays were not unusual in our postal system!)

In response to my accuser, I showed I had heard his words, but could only reiterate that I knew God had led me to the medical work at Lukolwe as a nurse in my own right and not merely to support any fellow workers who might be there, although we all needed one another.

That night I felt attacked in the extreme and very vulnerable, and yet was unable to 'go home and hide' in order to even think things through. It was close to midnight and I was a guest needing overnight accommodation with one of the single ladies. The return river crossing was far too dangerous to do at night unless it was an emergency. The next day the arduous crossing home seemed even longer than usual and it was well into the evening, after caring for the patients in our hospital, before I was able to sit down and examine the things said to me the night before.

I can remember just crying out to the Lord, longing to know His will. He was the One who had brought me to Lukolwe to serve the people of that community as a nurse and had, until now, not given me any indication I should leave. What did He want of me? Also, I had not yet had a direct reply from the elders in Zimbabwe and this indirect statement, given as though directly from them, had a feeling of falsehood about it. It just did not ring true to my contact with them up to that point. Kneeling by my bed, then on it inside the mosquito net, a long time was spent communing with a loving heavenly Father that night. I was able to ask Him to show me any truths in what had been said and what He wanted of me for the future.

Having committed that to Him I was able to lie down and sleep soundly after resolving to continue the work I had been doing, until such a time as there was further clarity. During those days it was easy to feel lonely and vulnerable, and this was made even harder because I did not feel I could share what had been said to me. That was true both with my fellow missionaries, as it would cause them even further pain and distress, or with any of my friends in the local community, as it would have raised anxiety and fear and perhaps even more bitterness around what were the already public divisions among the missionaries and some of the local churches.

It was probably at least two weeks later before the postal system brought the letter from the elders in Zimbabwe. During that time I had continued to live and work as normal with full days, and often night calls for maternity or sick people. Opening that letter on my own was hard, but it was so encouraging. They had felt I had replied to their queries fully and were satisfied that the rumours they were hearing did not affect the work I was doing. They finished with a statement that I had their full blessing, encouragement and continued prayer. Leaders of the other sending churches with whom I was in contact later also confirmed those words. Continuing to work in the place where God had sent me was refreshing.

Travel tales

Lukolwe was surrounded by huge flat areas, which were the flood plains feeding into the Zambezi River. These were many miles across, with the villages built on the fairly widely dispersed slightly raised areas. In the dry season the plains were dry sandy surfaces covered in grass which grew up to a couple of metres high. Later in the year many of these dry grasslands would burn off, with fires racing across them at enormous speed. Then when the rains came they flooded, and they could be up to a metre deep in water. All three seasons provided different challenges for the driver.

Lorne made a very special Heath Robinson-style adaptation for my Land Cruiser by adding a metre-long V of wood to the front bumper. By sticking out that far in front of the vehicle it fairly effectively divided the high grass, throwing most of the grass seed out to the sides. Without this adaptation, the seeds blocked the radiator very rapidly and the vehicle overheated. Even with it and at least two protective layers of fine gauze filter, the radiator had to be cleared of seeds all too frequently, a very fiddly task.

When the grass was very dry it was quite possible to be caught in the middle of such a plain, with smoke indicating a bush fire, and nowhere to flee. More than once it was necessary to start our own fire against the wind direction and burn off a patch of grass, then drive the vehicle and ourselves onto the burned-back area to await the main fire coming roaring through. After such fires, driving was easier as we could actually see the ground over which we were travelling!

During the flood season the plains were impossible to cross with a vehicle. Even when the water was fairly shallow, the ground became treacherous under the wheels and it was easy to become stuck. Thus at that time of the year we resorted to walking, or pushing a laden bicycle through the flooded areas to run clinics in the villages on the other side of a flood plain.

For the local population it became a time of abundance. As mentioned earlier, when the flood waters rose, fish eggs, safely hidden in the sand since the previous year, would hatch into tiny fish and provide an abundant supply of protein for the local population. The fish were caught in home-made baskets, then dried in the sun. They fed the family, and in truly abundant years also provided enough dried fish to send out to town for sale, giving an income to be used in leaner times.

By the time I left the area, the roads out to town were improved to the point where some of the men could make the trip, in good weather, in about twelve hours' hard driving. I preferred to make an overnight stop on the way. On my first trip (in 1965) it took us three days to reach Lukolwe. The first night we spent at Loloma Mission, which was my first contact with those who worked there. Loloma was almost exactly halfway from the Copperbelt to Lukolwe, so provided a very helpful point to break the journey after about nine hours of driving. The second night was spent at Dipalata Mission and we went on to Chavuma, then crossed the Zambezi River for the final leg the following morning.

Distances were often measured in hours rather than kilometres or miles. Having been in three different countries when they changed to the metric system of weights and measures, including Zambia, I had become bilingual regarding the actual measurement of distances. Thus it was no problem envisaging either miles or kilometres, but often a journey was planned far more with regard to the time that it would take if all went well, and then extra time was added for any hitches that probably would occur. An example of this would be the journey to Lusaka. Usually we travelled via the Copperbelt, but there was another route we could use. That saved about 350km (just over 200 miles) in distance, but the rural tracks, uncertain ferry crossings and so on meant the journey would take as long, if not longer, over poorer roads.

Trips to town continued to be demanding, and several of our fellow missionaries died on those roads, including Vi Collias, who had been one of the first people I met when landing in Balovale airport on my first visit to the area. A very experienced driver, she was driving out to town accompanied by a friend from Chitokoloki, to take two visiting young schoolteachers from Wales out for their flight home. They literally just seemed to vanish. The teachers, who were sisters, had been helping at Sakeji School, and then journeyed to our area for a visit before returning home. The previous night they had slept in my house, then travelled down to Chitokoloki in preparation for leaving early the following morning. No one knows how or why the vehicle left the road, hit a tree, burst into flames and was incinerated. We will never know the answer. When no news was heard of their safe arrival on the Copperbelt, the two husbands set off to find them and were the first to realise that a terrible accident had happened. Such occurrences shook us all and left us feeling very vulnerable.

One journey I made was very unusual in that, for some reason, I was completely alone in the Land Cruiser and was driving on a Sunday. About 600km from the start of the journey, in an apparently isolated section of the road, a rear tyre went flat. The roads were made of laterite, a reddish clay material, and it had recently stopped raining. They were also steeply cambered, not the best surface for changing a tyre! In dismay I stopped and went to look at the offending wheel. Before I could do anything about it, a man dressed in his Sunday best suit stopped and offered to help. Within minutes another, equally smartly attired, joined him. Between them they changed the heavy wheel, stowed away the damaged one, and the three of us stood in the middle of the road trying to wash the red mud off our hands in a puddle. Between us, we represented three different tribes, spoke at least four languages, but could only communicate by gestures. The men's suits were covered in staining red mud, and when I offered them something for their help, they both refused with clear indications that we were all one in Christ Jesus. They had both been on their way home from church services in different villages.

On another trip I was driving back from the town with a ton of goods on the trailer, and a half-ton load in the back of the Land Cruiser, when there was a flat tyre. That time was shortly after the accident in which the four ladies died and we were about thirty minutes short of Loloma. We stopped the vehicle, and the workmen with me were just beginning to unload it to reach a spare tyre when a crowd of people arrived from a nearby unseen village. They greeted me joyfully by my African name, chased the workmen off, and proceeded to change our tyre and have us back on the road within about ten minutes. This was so unexpected! It was a village with many Christians who had attended Bible camps at Lukolwe. They would have fed us, too, but understood when we explained why we needed to reach the two-way radio at Loloma before broadcast-time in order to reassure others that we were safe. We arrived there with minutes to spare.

Flat tyres were common, particularly when there was a heavy load. It was routine to carry several spare wheels for both the pickup and the trailer. Each wheel and tyre weighed about seventy-five pounds so they were not easy to handle.

On another trip I collected a new Toyota Land Cruiser in Cape Town, had a canopy fitted on the back, then drove from Cape Town up to Harare to visit my mother, before continuing on to Zambia. As I have mentioned earlier, I had picked up a friend, Ruth, in Johannesburg, so had company on the journey. Because the Zimbabwe–Zambia border was closed at that time owing to sanctions against Zimbabwe, we had to go the long way around. It added about another 1,100km to the already 3,622km journey (about 3,000 miles total), and additional actual driving time of more than twenty-five hours as we drove back south to Bulawayo, then up to Victoria Falls. From there we went along the border with Botswana, into Namibia and on to the Kasengula ferry crossing over the Zambezi River.

We enjoyed a few daylight hours at Victoria Falls, spent the night there and next morning left before 5am, setting off westwards along the isolated dirt road to Kasengula. Ruth and I began to think that a pit stop would be a good idea. We were rolling to a halt without braking when a leopard walked slowly out from the side of the road and crossed within about 2m of the front of the Toyota, climbed the bank and stood there looking with interest at us in the, by then, stationary vehicle. It was magnificent and so graceful. Needless to say we both decided not to exit the vehicle right then!

The crossing is at a point where four countries meet, Zimbabwe, Zambia, Botswana and the Caprivi Strip of Namibia. The journey took us through the numerous border posts, onto the huge ferry at Kasengula and across the river into Zambia.

Another time when Nicki was returning to Zambia after her midwifery training, I drove out to Lusaka to meet her at the airport. From there we drove east and up into the Luangwa National Park. This added an extra twenty-two hours driving to our journey home, but what a wonderful time we had there. When we arrived we found a group of very serious ministers from the German Lutheran Church had gathered and were using the lodges for meetings. The two of us were the only other visitors staying in the lodges. We were saddened to realise that the men, dressed completely in black, were only focused on their meetings and apparently had little or no interest in the wonderful world and wildlife around them.

But we benefited in an unexpected way when Norman Carr, the manager of the whole park, took the two of us under his wing and we had special trips out each day, sometimes into the closed-off areas of the park. He was a world-renowned wildlife expert, and shared with us his love of the animals, understanding of their lives, and much more.

One day he took us even further afield as he went to look for a massive male lion which had been badly injured in a poacher's trap. Care had been taken of the lion for many weeks, and he was provided with meat until he was able to hunt for himself again. Having been left in his natural environment throughout his recovery, the wardens had gone out to him regularly. For us it was thrilling to be so close, in the vehicle, to a fully maned wild adult lion as he rested under a tree. His neck wound was almost healed and Norman threw him a huge chunk of meat, satisfied he was recovering well. Norman also took us on trips where he taught us to recognise the many birds, the spoor of different animals, how they lived and much, much more. Then in the evenings we were able to sit in the lodge area overlooking a pool at which many animals, large and small, came to drink. It was a restful and very enjoyable short holiday and a much-appreciated time for Nicki and myself to renew our relationship.

Norman certainly shared with us his passion for that unique wilderness. He died in 1997, having spent most of his life in the game conservation areas of Zambia.

For the first five years at Lukolwe I did not own a vehicle, and emergencies were usually covered by use of one of the vehicles owned by the two families with whom I worked.

Many of the stories already told make reference to an essential and often life-saving vehicle. By that time both families had five children, and for one of them, when the older boys reached secondary school level, they had to make the difficult decision to move to where the children could receive the education they needed. For missionary parents, this is often a very hard time as they face the needs of their family and the demands of the work into which they believed God had led them. One family stayed at Lukolwe and the children were home-schooled by correspondence. The other family decided to move.

One day John came to me and said, 'As we agreed, you have first refusal of our four-wheel drive vehicle.' This was a surprise, as I had not even thought of the possibility of my owning a vehicle. After talking it over with the Lord, and a considerable inner struggle, as I did not believe in going into debt, I agreed to buy the vehicle, knowing it would be essential for the medical work. The price was set at a certain figure, with the proviso that it might be changed after they had been out to the town and researched the value of such a Toyota Land Cruiser.

After a trip to town, the price was increased by £500, which was a lot of money in those days. It took another conscious step of faith to trust the Lord for the increased amount, but having made the commitment I was at peace. Also, we made an agreement that I would pay them the balance of the money as and when I had it available and, in the meanwhile, if anything happened to myself and the vehicle (our roads were very dangerous), they could not turn to my parents for the balance of the funds.

That family left us late November, and by the end of December, the cost had been paid in full. I had told no one of the purchase, and even if I had written about it, the postal system could not have brought a reply from anyone in less than six weeks. But that month I received three particular gifts from Christians across the world. One was £1,000 from the UK, one $1,000 from the USA, and the third K1,000 from someone in Zambia. All of these people had responded to God's prompting without any knowledge of why there was a need, and the gifts were all one-offs from people who had never sent money previously, and did not do so again.

This was probably the only time that needs were met in such a dramatic way, but throughout the twenty-five years I was at Lukolwe, every financial need was met for myself and for the medical work. There was no promise of a regular amount on which to live, with the exception of one church who committed themselves to a small amount monthly when I first went there. An unexpected change in circumstances, because of war and isolation for them, meant that regular amount was only available for about six months and then stopped completely. But the loving heavenly Father, who sent me out to that isolated place, provided all that was necessary through his Christian people.

He even went further, and without my knowledge, some of the ladies in the church in Cape Town chose to put into a special account a small amount every month towards my 'retirement years'. They began in 1965, when I first went to Lukolwe, and faithfully contributed throughout the following twenty-five years. That money later was brought over here to England, and played a large part in the purchase of the home in which I have now lived for many years.

Turning around

Recently a friend shared a story that reminded me of what happened many years ago, when God really spoke to me and showed me I was displeasing Him. She commented that God does not dilly-dally when He wants to alert us to what He is saying, but uses powerful means to do so. That was so true for me that day!

All those years ago, I was carrying all the responsibilities of the medical work and the demands that were part of daily living at Lukolwe, and was very stressed. I was becoming more and more angry at the way that the staff, who had only minimal training, were failing to maintain the standards I thought were necessary. Every day seemed a struggle and I was not happy about it, but it just seemed part of the pressure of life and living at that time. One of the main problems was myself, but I didn't recognise it.

One day a loving Christian friend came alongside and pointed out to me that my attitude was breaking down relationships with the local people, particularly with my staff, who were very unhappy about the pressure that this was causing for all of them. They were asking why I had gone there as God's servant, but was making life so hard for them. My response was a painful one. I felt threatened, afraid, exposed and in some ways probably betrayed. But most of all I felt a failure. The conviction that God had sent me to Lukolwe as His servant was still as clear as it had been, but by my actions I had endangered that and dishonoured Him.

As I talked with the Lord about it, I began to realise that the issue was around my anger. It was displeasing to the Lord, displeasing to my staff and displeasing to myself. I hadn't recognised it until that friend came alongside me and pointed out the error of my ways. He went as far as to say that some in the community were beginning to wonder whether it was worth my while working there because it was making life so uncomfortable for the people around me. I was completely ashamed.

I didn't understand the situation, didn't understand myself, but I knew that my loving heavenly Father put me there for that work. That assurance, that realisation was very clear. He had sent me there, but I was not honouring Him. What a struggle those days were. They did indeed seem very dark. In the ongoing conversation with the Lord, as I read His Word and realised the depth of my failure, I was able to lay it out before Him and ask His forgiveness. I began to recognise that it wasn't the anger as such that was the problem, it was the way I was handling it. It was the way I related to the people around me. Also another issue was that running the hospital was God's work, not mine, I was only the servant.

Was this the end of my life and work at Lukolwe?

There were some particular incidents where I recognised I had been wrong and, after first asking the Lord's forgiveness and His help to really change, went individually to the members of staff concerned, apologising for the way I had spoken to them and asking for their forgiveness too. I think in some ways I was expecting that God would then make things right immediately. He had made it so obvious, so clear, and I had repented. So now He would change me and turn it all around so that it would be a time of honouring Him and I would be able to overcome this anger ... But I was to learn that it was a daily commitment, a moment-by-moment walk with the Lord, that was needed. At first it seemed that so many times each day I was recognising issues and constantly asking His forgiveness for the way I'd spoken.

Several days into this exercise of learning, I again spoke abruptly to a member of staff when he had not met the standards that I had been setting. I remember then going into the small pharmacy to be alone. The door was open and I just talked to the Lord, asking His forgiveness, and said, 'Lord, please forgive me again, I just seem to be constantly blowing it.'

It was as though He spoke to me and said, 'What do you mean *again*? This is the first time, as far as I'm concerned. Anything in the past has gone because I have cleansed it; this is the only thing that needs forgiving.' It was as though a light came on. I realised that it was as if, outside that door, there was no longer that whole heap of sin, a whole heap of failure that I couldn't get past. It was all gone and was clean and clear. It was only for this episode that I needed forgiveness.

Somehow that made a huge difference. Over the next few days of intense consciousness of needing the Lord's help, very gradually and with decreasing frequency each day, the negative responses dissipated and over a few weeks things began to settle down.

Then in the middle of one night I was called over to the maternity room for a mother having her first baby. The maternity nurse on duty, a lovely local Christian lady, trained by myself but limited by little actual education, was working with me. The patient's grandmother was with her granddaughter for support during her labour. At some point I became aware that the nurse had done something (or not done something) that had the potential to endanger the mother or the new baby, and was upset. Instead of just commenting or rebuking her, I was angry and I spoke strongly with harsh words to her in front of the patient and her relative.

The new baby arrived safely and both were tucked away in their beds. We cleared up and went back to our houses to have a few hours sleep. But I couldn't sleep, because once again I had blown it! Once again I had spoken in a way that wasn't honouring to God. That morning I knelt by my bed and talked to the Lord about it, first asking for His forgiveness, His cleansing. Then I knew it was my responsibility to go back and ask forgiveness from the maternity nurse. She was hard at work when I found her, and I did indeed ask forgiveness for the way I spoken to her and for the fact that I had done it in front of other people. I then added the reminder that she knew that what she did was wrong and could have endangered our patient. My Christian sister forgave me that day. She heard the rebuke and accepted it, but she also knew that I genuinely wanted her forgiveness for the harsh and public words spoken. This resulted in a stronger relationship between us in the days, months and years ahead. But it was a sharp reminder to me that perhaps I had begun to be complacent. I had started to see change and accept it and be less aware of the danger, and it brought me back to kneeling before the Lord. Indeed, His 'strength is made perfect in weakness' (2 Corinthians 12:9, KJV).

The follow-on to this made such a difference because some months later Nicki came out to live and work with me. After she'd been there for several months, a comment came up in our conversation in which I said something to her about my being 'an angry person'. She turned to me, looking astonished, commenting that she had never seen me angry. That came from someone who lived and worked with me each day. What a challenge and encouragement that was to me and what a reminder to thank my heavenly Father for all that He had done.

It wasn't until something which happened many months later made clearer still the lesson that had been learned. I had become ill. As mentioned earlier, my white cell blood count was extremely low and I had been ordered by the doctor to be flown out as an emergency the 3,200km to Cape Town for medical care. I had been warned that the illness could result in my death, and even if I recovered it was extremely unlikely I would ever return to Lukolwe. It was arranged that the AEF Cessna plane was to be flown in to our grass airstrip from one of the other missions late that afternoon. The pilot was going to spend the night at Lukolwe and we were to take off as the sun rose at seven o'clock the next morning, 1st August 1984. Nicki was travelling with me as I was very weak and needed her support. Meanwhile we had to prepare the staff at the hospital and ensure adequate supplies of medication for both patients and staff, enabling them to manage as well as possible without the support of both the trained nurses.

Because of vulnerability to infection, I had been forbidden to go near people. Nicki and I went over to the hospital early that morning and I sat in the empty examination room, with the door open and looking out across the hospital. Despite the physical weakness, I was able to help Nicki remember the things needing to be done in preparation before we left. She had to return to the house for something, leaving me on my own. Sitting looking out over that hospital, I talked with the Lord. I can remember saying something such as, 'Father, it is Your hospital and I can trust you. I've been here for twenty years and failed many times but have done my best. Thank you Father, for the knowledge that I can leave it to You, knowing You are in control. It is Your hospital, not mine, and as we leave tomorrow morning it is in Your hands.' I was filled with the most wonderful peace. The Bible talks about a peace that 'passes all understanding' (Philippians 4:7, RSV) and I think that day I knew a special measure of that peace as I looked out on the place that had been my home for so long.

It was only then that I saw that incident about my anger in a new light. I suddenly realised that because of the struggle that I had been through many months previously, the odds had changed. Up to that point, the hospital had been 'mine' and my responsibility. I believed that the work had been mine and I had to keep it going. The stress had been too much. Somehow in the months since then, that had changed – from the hospital being *my* hospital, *my* responsibility, to being *God's* hospital, *His* responsibility, and myself His servant in that place – and that was why I could trust Him. That was why I could know such peace in walking away, possibly never to return, because He was in control.

It was a number of years later before I also understood more clearly that the anger I was demonstrating in those stressful days had been modelled in me from childhood. Through my mother I had learned that the automatic response to pressure was anger. At the time of working through those black days, I had no concept of this, but coming to the understanding of the source of my 'inbuilt' response to stress helped me to recognise it, and to accept and deal with it in a new way. That understanding in turn helped me later on to work with other issues in life.

In God's goodness He restored my health and enabled me to return to Lukolwe for a further five years. But from that day forward the work was never so stressful in the way that it had been before, as I continued to learn this lesson. It was His hospital and I could trust Him for the stresses and strains. Oh yes, there were times again when I tried working out issues in my own strength, but recognised it much earlier and was able to ask forgiveness and hand them back to God, understanding something of His greater plan. And then when it came to the time when He showed me I should finally leave Lukolwe (in 'my plan' I was prepared to live there for the rest of my life), I was able to lay down that responsibility with a quiet heart and trust Him to continue what He had started.

Instead of my looking at it all as 'my work for God', and therefore my ultimate responsibility, I realised that it was God's work with which I had been entrusted. When things were tough, He actually had the answers! During all those twenty-five, often very difficult, years it was at those times when I tried to cope in my own strength (Oh yes, I constantly prayed and cried to Him, but ...) that the stress levels rose to unmanageable proportions and I lost objectivity and the ability to see God's bigger picture. I just wish that it had not needed such a radical way to make me listen!

God's leading ...

In 2009 I was praying and thinking about what to share with a group of ladies. As I wondered about which passage to choose, I kept coming back to times when God has shown me the way forward through His Word.

What does being led by God from His Word really look like? How does it work out in our daily lives? Is the Word of God relevant in big decisions, but not so relevant in the daily issues? Can the Bible tell us exactly what decision to make every time we read it?

No, we are not given exact instructions. He expects us to take responsibility for our daily lives and use the wisdom He has given us and the principles shown in His Word.

> Guard what has been entrusted to your care.
> (1 Timothy 6:20)

Through the years I have learned that God's Word is alive and speaks into my current situation. But it was rarely that one verse stood out totally in the context of my daily reading. It can happen that a verse previously memorised will come back into my mind in unexpected places, but that too is unusual.

I would like to share some of those memorable times when God has spoken through His written Word and this has led to life-changing actions.

> Rejoice in the Lord always. I will say it again: rejoice! Let your gentleness be evident to all. The Lord is near. Do not be anxious about anything, but in every situation, by prayer and petition, with thanksgiving, present your requests to God. And the peace of God, which transcends all understanding, will guard your hearts and your minds in Christ Jesus.
> (Philippians 4:4-7)

God's peace (verse 7) – has two dates written beside it in my Bible – 3 October 1980 and 16 August 1983. After the second one I had written, 'In faith to remain at Lukolwe'. I had had a real struggle as things were just too hard, my fellow workers were saying they were returning to the United States and I would have been the only expatriate worker left there. After hours of struggling with God I had finally said, 'Right, Lord, Your will be done – I will stay, whatever the pressures.' My heart was filled with that peace and I lay down and slept soundly. A few months later He sent Nicki to join me.

One day I was reading in Romans and the last phrase of the last verse stood out: '… and everything that does not come from faith is sin' (Romans 14:23). That has had a profound impact on how I have viewed sin since that time. That day it was as though God said to me, 'Whatever does not please Me, is sin, and I want You to trust Me in every aspect of life, the routine and the unusual.'

Other days, when reading in the early morning, something in the passage has reminded me of someone else and the consciousness to pray for them has been powerful. But, too, there have been times when it has been a compulsion to go to them – and whenever I have obeyed, it has always been right.

Some of the big occasions are more easily remembered than the everyday situations, but those are no less important.

It was 1965, when I was considering going to work at Lukolwe in Zambia. Quite a lot had happened in the previous few months and I had become anxious about my own right understanding of God's will. At that point I had gone up to Zambia for a six-week visit and within days began to believe that indeed Lukolwe was the place God wanted me to be. But ... as shared earlier, I was anxious about the heat and my reading the next morning was Jeremiah 17:7-8.

Next to that passage I have a number of dates written in my Bible, the first being:

Aug 1965 – Promise for Lukolwe

That promise confirmed to me that God was in my move to Lukolwe, and as long as my trust and confidence was in Him it would work out even in the hot season.

Of course, I am human, and therefore through the years tried in my own strength too often, resulting in a growing fear of failure and of bearing no fruit. In my Bible next to the same text is also written the date: '25.9.83 No worries – *will bear fruit*'.

It was a time when I myself had not been as dependent on the Lord and things were not going very well – and the following verses stood out too:

> The heart is deceitful above all things and beyond cure. Who can understand it? 'I the LORD search the heart and examine the mind, to reward a man according to his conduct, according to what his deeds deserve.'
> (Jeremiah 17:9-10, NIV 1984)

I knew that Jeremiah 17:7-8 was the ultimate scripture God used to take me to Lukolwe, and was prepared to stay there for the rest of my life, if that was what He wanted. Twenty-five years later it was another passage in Jeremiah that He used in a different way to tell me it was time to move on. I was at Lukolwe for the long haul and one of my strengths is stickability – but like most strengths, it can also become a weakness. It took God three separate occasions to get one message through to me – that it was time for a change.

In January 1989 I had had malaria lasting more than six weeks and the final drugs I took as treatment had left me unable to walk, even to the bathroom. I felt awful. My reading that day was:

'For I know the plans I have for you,' declares the LORD, 'plans to prosper you and not to harm you, plans to give you hope and a future.'
(Jeremiah 29:11)

At that point, for whatever reason, the words made a deep impact on me, although as I read them that morning lying on my bed, it seemed the promise was simply that I would recover from the malaria and survive!

As previously arranged with the elders of a church in Northwood that had been supporting me since 1984, I came over to the UK in March. One Sunday a lady whom I scarcely knew came up to me during the service with her open Bible in her hand and said, 'I have never done this before, but I believe that God wants me to point out this verse to you.' She pointed to Jeremiah 29:11 and I noted it and later read the next few verses too. But I still did not understand that God was moving me forward. As far as I was concerned I was in the UK for three months, then returning to Lukolwe.

In July, when I was visiting a church in Exeter exactly the same thing happened. Another lady came to me and pointed out the same verse. Again it was a place where God's people had been praying for me and supporting me for many years. By now I had begun to really take notice. What was God saying?

During the time in the UK, extended from three to six months because of medical investigations into the cause of renal colic and kidney stones from which I had been suffering, God had given me a home. It was a roomy maisonette near the church in Northwood. So many unexpected and wonderful things happened in the choice of and then purchase of the maisonette, that I had no doubt it was in God's control. Although very thankful for it, in my thinking it was an investment for my far-off retirement – should I ever retire at all! However, it could be rented out to students attending the nearby London Bible College. At that point I had no thought of using it myself in the near future.

But as I travelled around the local areas on my bicycle, visiting many folk and involved in the pastoral care in the local church, something happened that startled me. I began to have a deep desire to serve the people of this area of Northwood. From my early twenties that inner desire had been focused only on Lukolwe and the people of that part of Zambia, so this was a new and challenging change.

Once that change began to actually reach my mind and heart, it was discussed with the church elders, friends at Echoes of Service, etc, and gradually a deep peace came into my heart that it was the right time for me to leave Lukolwe and return to England permanently.

I mentioned my health needs had kept me here for an extra three months. During that time the decision was made to return to Lukolwe for only five months in order to sort things out and say goodbye. About ten days before I was due to leave Northwood and return to Zambia, the phone rang at 10.30pm. It was from the professor of medicine at the Royal London Hospital telling me that they had found some of the cause of my medical problems and his advice to me was that I should not return to the tropics to stay for more than five months.

Wow! Having reached that timing myself, what a confirmation was given through that lovely Christian medical advisor, who had known nothing of the decision I had already made.

Guidance is not an easy thing and we often need clarity for major changes, although principles guide us day by day. Believing guidance often has five aspects: God's Word, the desires of one's heart, circumstances, godly Christian advice through people you respect spiritually, and a special peace deep in one's heart.

All those aspects came into making the final decision that it was time to leave Lukolwe and come and live in Northwood, in the UK. Because that was the case, I have never doubted that it was God's plan for me. The decision was hard, and well I remember the tears on the day I finally drove away from the place and people who had been so precious to me for so long, but through it all that deep supernatural peace held my heart secure.

Leaving Lukolwe

Knowing that I was leaving Lukolwe, I was determined to spend time in saying goodbye. Many other missionaries had come and gone through the years and so many people of the area had lamented the lack of opportunity to say goodbye. I had been there for twenty-five years, it was my home and the farewells were necessary for me as well as those I was leaving. That decision proved to be a very blessed one for us all. I had hoped one day to return for a visit, but up to now my health has not allowed that.

After returning there in September 1989 I sought to tell all the leaders of the area in person about my leaving, and also visited various isolated areas. The overall response was one of genuine grief and sorrow. There were some people I was unable easily to meet in person and so I wrote to them.

In response, a Christian Luvale chief from Litapi, about 80km away, wrote asking me to make a trip out there to say goodbye. As the rainy season had started and the plains between Lukolwe and Litapi would flood very soon, thereby making the journey impossible by vehicle, I set out with four Luvale friends on 29th December 1989.

We had planned a round trip via Litapi, and on to Nguvu and Nyatanda, visiting five different groups of Christians. The whole trip would be less than 240km, but took us about seventeen hours of actual driving time!

Besides my bedding roll, preparations for the trip were minimal – two saucepans, plates, spoons, salt, a mixture of milk powder and sugar, cocoa, a little local millet meal for porridge (just in case we needed it – not used), and a couple of onions! Of course, the vehicle had more attention, and contained the necessary survival equipment such as a winch, spade, jacks, axe – all of which were used, plus flasks of hot water for coffee! I was accompanied by several Christian friends – Mavis, a lovely young mother with her small baby, as well as an older lady called Uliya, and Josiah Ngiza (an evangelist) and his wife.

My colleague had a newish project to increase food production by growing rice. The day before our leaving on the trip, some queries arose regarding the rice farm and the need for more seed rice. As we would be passing the farm, 42km out on the Kaxiji flood plain, I agreed to take out four 90kg bags of seed rice. They were huge. By the time the team, some six bags of corn meal for food for the workmen in the rice fields, our bedding, two extra women who had asked for a lift, a maternity patient with newborn baby and two-year-old child going home, were all packed into the back of the Land Cruiser, it was not easy to close the doors. Leaving Lukolwe, we travelled over a locally built wooden bridge across the Muyeke River, through a village and out onto the open plain.

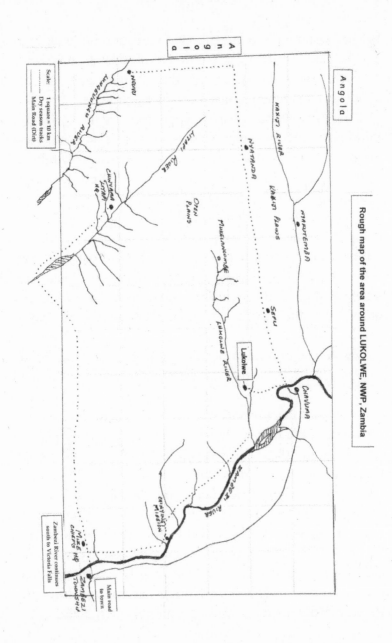

Rough map of the area around LUKOLWE, NWP, Zambia

How can one describe a plain to someone who has never seen it? Miles and miles of what looks like sandy flat grassland, with only the very occasional stunted bush, or small clump of trees on slightly higher ground. Over it one follows two wheel marks of varying clarity, crisscrossed occasionally by other footpaths. As the grass begins to grow, the tracks are often only seen if you are looking at the correct angle, by the slightly different shimmer on the surface of the grass that grows over them. The apparently flat grassland reveals itself to hold many traps for the unwary – bumps and lumps, twists and turns, small hard anthills, old stumps, holes dug by someone looking for small animals for food ... and so on. All the plains are flooded in the rainy season.

We reached the farm and, to our passengers relief, unloaded the rice and corn meal. Following a short discussion regarding the work being done, we set off once again towards Litapi. The journey, although slow, passed easily as Josiah and I chatted about spiritual things. He was the team leader for the Zambezi area, and a lovely godly and wise man. In fact, our discussions were so interesting that we forgot to stop and pick local wild fruits on the plain, and so earned a rebuke from the ladies! We almost forgot to collect and cut some logs for firewood, but thankfully remembered that in time, as there is very little firewood at Litapi.

Arriving at the church, a mud-brick and grass thatched building, we were met by a Christian who directed us to an empty house in the health centre complex which had been prepared for us. Truly we were received with joy, and our every need was supplied. The Christians there cared for us in every way. One lovely lady gave all of her time to cooking the abundance of food given to us (eighteen fresh fish, three live chickens, rice for breakfast, corn meal and cassava meal) and caring for us in other ways. Others drew water, and we were presented with a basin of hot water to bathe twice a day. The love and concern was tremendous, and I delighted to be treated as they would treat one of their own people – in this case, an important one, as they desired to show their gratitude for the years of caring they had received. The only work I did was to extract a difficult and infected tooth for one of the men. That earned us the gift of yet another chicken!

One concession to comfort was to take a deckchair and cushion for my own use – it tore within ten minutes! Low, locally made stools are back-breaking. A thin mattress on the floor was rather harder than my usual bed, but the mosquito net protected me from the bedbugs that proved to be in the house. My friends slept on a canvas on the floor, and not only had a hard bed, but were badly bitten that first night. The local Christians came to sing hymns together during the evening and, with Josiah preaching, they only finished after 11pm. We were weary, and I was unhappy about the long sermon, but felt ashamed of my response later when three different people told us how it had spoken to their hearts. The next night we were all relieved when the rain stopped the singing at 10pm!

It was a treat to eat an abundance of bream, as fresh fish are very rare at Lukolwe, and the *shima* was well made. The initial three live chickens were the start of a collection of eight given as gifts along the way, and as the women bought a further four, we had a collection of twelve by the time we returned. They would make tasty meals, although tough, but did add another complication to the transport situation. They were all safely kept in locally produced basket-style containers tied to the roof rack of the Land Cruiser.

Saturday afternoon there was a gathering in the church to say goodbye. A ninety-minute sermon followed a time of singing. It was an excellent message, but I would have preferred it given over several sessions! Yet for the people there it was a rare opportunity for them to receive such teaching and Josiah made the most of it. I then shared with them how God was leading me into new ways, and found real encouragement both in their words and in their prayers as they said goodbye.

Sunday saw us up and tentatively planning to be away by 6.30am so that we could meet with other Christians at Winela Church. But it was village life where time is different. Many Litapi friends came to say farewell and sing us on our way. They walked besides the vehicle singing all the way to the chief's enclosure and then while we went into the chief's palace. Before leaving the palace, a summons came through a court messenger. The local Member of Parliament had arrived at the rest house late the previous evening and wished to see me before we left. It was after 8.30am before we finally were on the way.

Ahead lay another twenty-two miles of 'bush' driving to the isolated area we were to visit. Not the plains this time, but open ground covered by stunted bushes and areas of swamp. The bumps seemed endless and being waved down as we drove through an isolated village was almost a relief. Help was wanted for the removal of several loose teeth. These were duly extracted, and we were presented with one very small chicken and some pineapples. On again right to the eastern border of Angola where we reached the next area, Nguvu (called 'hippopotamus' after all the hippos in the local river). There the men were just beginning to gather for the service. All the women were out in the 'masangu' (Bullrush millet) fields keeping the many birds off their crops.

After arranging to return and say farewell, we collected one of the men to direct us and set off to cross the river plain and the huge Lungevungu River to Winela. A mere two hundred yards later we were firmly stuck in a muddy stream. It took about an hour, much work, and the use of the powerful Toyota winch to pull us out. The drive across the river plain was otherwise uneventful except for the stress on the driver, as I felt anxious when driving through water and mud. The implications of being stuck are hair-raising, although we always managed eventually to get out. The last time we had been stuck in an isolated area it had taken more than four hours to free the vehicle.

We sat chatting on the banks of the river until the small canoe, carved from a tree trunk, was brought to fetch us. Mavis was afraid, as she had never crossed in such a manner before and there were many crocodiles and hippos in that deep, fast-flowing river, but we arrived safely and were warmly greeted by the Christian men. Again most women were out in the millet and rice fields working hard to provide their food for the coming year. They literally had to be continually chasing the birds off the developing grain, or in just a couple of hours their whole crop could have been eaten down to the last seed. The red-billed quelea birds arrive in huge flocks, eat until all the seed has gone and then leave for the next available field.

The people really appreciated the effort to reach them, and I was much encouraged by the time there. Back across the river, and another short time stuck in the mud on the plain, and we arrived back at Nguvu. The re-crossing of the muddy stream was nerve-racking, but I managed to get the Toyota across despite very, very nearly sinking into the mud again.

Spending a while with the Christians was good. They had prepared some food for us. By that time it was 4pm and we had only had a few mangoes since rice at 6.15am, so we needed and enjoyed the meal. Yet it was not without interest as very heavy rain started just as we began to eat, and the roof leaked badly. We spent the meal dodging the drips, which also fell in the relish, the *shima*, and plop, plop, plop into our glasses of water. Village life in the rain can be rather difficult, and we all had damp beds that night.

Running from the house to the car had us soaked through, but that is not too unpleasant when the heat is so great, and we soon dried out. The next three hours were spent travelling over another bumpy plain with the rain keeping just ahead of us all the way. About fifteen miles from the nearest village we came across an elderly man in a soaked overcoat, with his bundle on a stick over his shoulder. He was very grateful for a lift!

At Nyatanda we received a cheerful welcome, although circumstances were far from easy for the folk there. The house in which we were to stay, Josiah's own home, had been used by his sons to store their rice harvest. As a result it was not only full of rice, but rats too. There were too many of us to sleep in one room, so finally Josiah pitched his small tent for himself and his wife, and the rest of us spread out on the floor of the only available room. His new roof was dry but the rain kept up all night and as every action meant going outside, whether it was cooking in the kitchen shelter, drawing water, going to the latrine or unloading the car, it made life wet!

The local villages were apparently empty. An influenza epidemic had hit the area about a week earlier and in some villages every person was prostrate. In many, only one person was more or less on their feet and caring for the others. A few of the men were learning that a woman's work is hard! I had never before seen a village area so severely affected, but none had yet died and it seemed to be lasting four or five days, followed by a slow improvement. The local clinic had no medicines, not even aspirin. We shared what little we had, but it did not go far.

The next day a few gathered at the house to bid me farewell, and their love and care were very real. One young man reminded me that when I had come to Lukolwe God had brought me, and although I had known no one here, I had found friends and 'relatives'. The same God was now leading me away from here but He would continue to care for me in the future.

Seven miles further on we arrived at our last port of call, although the journey home held four more stops to meet the needs of different folk. This time the welcome was overwhelming. We had eaten at Nyatanda, but had to eat more rice here. There were gifts of chickens, rice, fruit and even cash. The Christians had prepared a number of songs to sing, words to encourage, and they generally showed their love, and grief. Their farewell act was to walk alongside the car singing for half a mile or further, and it was very emotional.

The whole trip was very worthwhile, and we were thankful to arrive home at dusk, having had no problems with the vehicle, only been badly stuck once, and all healthy. It was a time of uplifting and encouragement, and also refreshing as a much-needed break from the many tasks I faced each day. Despite the physical exhaustion, I am so glad that we went.

Farewell meeting

Another task I really wanted to accomplish before leaving was the completion of a new hospital block for outpatients' work. It had been started prior to my visit to England and was nearing completion, constructed from concrete blocks and sisal-and-cement roofing tiles made on site. Compared to what had previously been used, it was to be far more user-friendly for both staff and patients. Our old building, which was constructed of mud and thatched, had been there for several years before I had arrived at Lukolwe a quarter of a century earlier. By 1990 it was too small, was impossible to keep clean and had served its time. My leaving date gave the impetus to complete the new building and I was delighted to actually see it in use.

When very near completion, the local government representative approached me and asked that we have an official opening ceremony. Overwhelmed with all that needed to be done, to me that just seemed a step too far, so my reply was that if the local community wanted to arrange it that would be fine, but I could not be part of the preparations. That was the reply they wanted as they had quietly planned it not so much to be an opening ceremony for the outpatients' building, but a farewell for me. When the day came, it was a surprise indeed!

Crowds of people walked many miles (and some for days) to be there and were probably several hundred strong. They had meticulously planned it all and besides the actual ceremony time, cattle were butchered, the women worked hard for days producing cassava flour (meal) and sufficient food was cooked to feed everyone. The government Minister for Health from Lusaka had travelled up in order to be present. The whole day was an emotional roller coaster for me and a very special time when I knew I was loved, valued, and would be missed.

They had planned various speakers, including the Minister of Health, Lorne Ferguson, our fellow missionary, and Sambaza – the church elder and dear friend I have mentioned before. Then he must have been at least 100 and hadn't spoken at any meeting for a long period. That was his last time, as he went to be with the Lord shortly after I left the area. But he was determined to speak that day and, in true African style, was not brief!

Many things were said. Things I had never dreamt of hearing from that community in which I had lived for so long. They had concluded that I was having to leave because of health reasons and that those had been a result of the work among them for all those years. They showed me how much they had seen Jesus through the work, love and care given, something that through the years I had often questioned in the pressures of overwork and unceasing demands. At one point they washed my feet as a token of how often I had 'washed their feet' in so many ways. The crowd roared their approval. Of course, the story of Jesus washing His disciples' feet was clearly presented, but I cannot remember much of what was actually said. It was so humbling.

NORTHWOOD
1990 onwards

Re-entry . . .

So, God had unexpectedly showed me that it was time to leave Lukolwe and return to the land of my birth – England. That was as clear as had been the original decision to go to Zambia and, although it was not easy, there was a deep peace that God's timing was perfect.

I thought that returning to live in the UK would make life easier. Yes, during many years at Lukolwe there had been great joys, but life had often been tough too – very tough. Yet coming back to settle in England was not simple. Not only was there a change of country, but of lifestyle, environment and almost every other aspect of living. Having been in Africa for more than forty-two years, that alone had huge implications, but during the last quarter of a century I had been living in very basic conditions in an isolated part of a tropical country, with huge responsibilities and a full-time job.

Suddenly life was a completely different shape. In some ways it *was* simpler. But even things like supermarkets felt rather threatening, with the volume of goods that were available and the choices that had to be made even for a single purchase. It was a change that I embraced because I was so sure that this was God's plan for me, but there were so many aspects that were actually far from easy.

The home I had been given even before I knew that I would be returning to Northwood was occupied by people from the local Bible school and their tenancy did not expire for several months. Because of the generosity and love of others, I had a roof over my head and was well cared for. But it still felt more as if I was on leave, as opposed to having moved into the new situation.

Another aspect was the fact that I had grown up from the age of seven in South Africa and Rhodesia, with their open-air, relaxed lifestyle and attitudes, followed by many years in a totally different environment and culture at Lukolwe. British culture felt like almost the opposite extreme, often leaving me bewildered in how to act and in how to relate to the interests of the society around me.

There was much to learn day by day. I have always enjoyed the challenge of learning new things, but as the months passed, the reality of a different lifestyle had to be embraced. New friendships and relationships had to be built. New ways discovered to cope with different situations; new dependencies built; new work found. Even relatively simple things such as using public transport or taxis felt stressful. And through it all I struggled with a deep tiredness that drained my energy. It was to be a long time, in fact many years, before we realised the cause of that enervating fatigue.

A new home

As mentioned earlier, my mother had died in 1984. Having no home away from Lukolwe, she wanted me to have a base, so had left me her town house in Harare. Thankfully, she never knew the changes in regulations enacted the very week she died. The authorities ruled that no one could own property in that country if not a Zimbabwean resident. Thus, in a very few weeks, Mum's home had to be emptied and sold. By law the money was then put into 4 per cent Zimbabwean bonds, with 25 per cent annual tax to be deducted, for the following twelve years. During those years it depreciated by about 90 per cent. But, when the time was right, God provided me with a new home in England.

I have shared above about the maisonette I had bought in Northwood. In 1989, when I was in the UK for three months, friends really encouraged me to consider buying a flat for when I retired. The interest on the money from my mother's home became the start of a down payment. At the time I was not too enthusiastic. After all, I was going to be at Lukolwe for the rest of my life! But under pressure from those friends I did look at a number of available flats. The ones we saw horrified me. They seemed so small. Being a tall person, often slightly uncoordinated, and having lived most of my life in rambling, open, spacious houses, those flats felt claustrophobic. It was discouraging in the extreme and I opted out of the search.

Then, one Sunday morning, as I was helping to serve refreshments after the church service, a lady came up to me and wanted to talk about a maisonette for sale where she lived. Being busy serving others, preoccupied and a bit impatient, I half-listened, but then we realised that both of us were invited to dinner at a mutual friend's house, so delayed the discussion. She made me feel under pressure to go to view this maisonette, but I was rather uncooperative, having decided not to 'flat hunt' any more and also reluctant to go amd look on a Sunday. After talking it through, I finally agreed to see the place with her during that afternoon, as it was literally just around the corner from our friends' home.

What an eye-opener! It was a large two-bedroom first-floor maisonette in very good condition. The owner was moving to the USA and wanted to sell it before leaving the following Wednesday, so had temporarily reduced the price by 15 per cent, bringing it almost within the price bracket I could manage. I arranged for a second viewing the next day, with another friend more experienced in the current UK property market. She marvelled at what she saw and was very encouraging, so we began to discuss an offer. The price came down another £2,000 as we would not be using an estate agent, but was still a full £2,000 over what I believed was the maximum that I could pay. Yet it was very good value at the asking price, and I was honest with the owner about the funding discrepancy.

Returning to our pastor's house where I was staying, I looked again at my bank accounts and talked with the Lord about the maisonette. Another Christian friend had arranged a low mortgage for me, a seeming impossibility as I had no fixed income. In my thinking the monthly payment would be covered by renting it out to Bible school students.

At that time very few people knew that I was even considering that purchase. I spent that evening with the friends who had encouraged me to look for a flat in the first place. The husband was the church treasurer and at the end of the evening he told how, when he came home from work, he had found an envelope on his mat containing a cheque as an anonymous gift for me. It was for £1,000. At that time, I was also holding the same amount of money for a school project in Zambia, but had been advised it would not be needed for at least twelve months. That night before going to bed I decided that the money held for the school computers could be used in the interim, and that it would be available again by the time it was needed.

Waking at 2am my heart was so filled with joy I wanted to shout and sing my praise at the certainty that God was in this. It was one of those special times. Then at 5am I quietly slipped out of the house, walked down to stand in the driveway, looking up at the maisonette and just talked to the Lord about it. This was such a big thing to be contemplating! But in my heart there was a deep peace.

Later that morning I again walked down to the maisonette and met the vendor as he was leaving to take bags of bits and pieces to the charity shop. Just minutes later and I would have missed him. We agreed to my purchasing the maisonette and he was delighted. He was a Jewish man and commented that through this sale he felt that God was blessing him as well. From first hearing about the maisonette until the agreement to the purchase had been literally forty-eight hours!

But the tale did not end there ...

When I returned home, the post had brought an unexpected letter. It was from the school, saying their plans had changed and requesting that the money be sent immediately. What was going on here? I talked to the Lord about it and decided not to mention the letter to anyone else at that time. Later that afternoon, stepping out in faith despite the shortfall, I went and signed the mortgage papers, before again visiting my friends from the previous evening. For a second time in two days they had had an envelope put through the door with an anonymous (to me) gift for ... yes, you will have guessed it, £1,000!

The Lord says, 'Before they call I will answer ...' (Isaiah 65:24).

The sale went through smoothly and within six weeks I moved into the maisonette, to fulfil regulations and live in it for a time before returning to Zambia. At that point I was still not considering any imminent possibility of returning to live permanently in the UK.

Without doubt God was in that purchase, and there is a very true sense in which He gave me the maisonette, despite my opposition to even looking at it. When, less than a year later, I returned to the UK to live, it was with the knowledge that God had provided for me before I even realised what I needed. And my prayer was that my new home would be a place used by the Lord for His people.

No work

On my return to live in Northwood I was faced with the challenge of finding a role in the working environment. From early on I worked as a pastoral carer with the church, but needed to find further paid employment as well. I had a small mortgage to pay monthly, which increased the pressure to find a job, but there seemed little available. My lifelong nursing and midwifery experience apparently counted for nothing and was looked upon as outdated because, according to the authorities, I had 'not practised as a nurse or midwife for twenty-five years'! That was despite all the work, training and research I had done through the years to maintain my skills and knowledge.

A friend pointed out an advert in a newspaper for an overnight carer needed for an elderly couple for two nights a week. It involved being in the house for two people who slept all night, having already been put to bed. It was nearby, so convenient, and I vividly remember throughout that first winter, trudging up the hill in the snow each Sunday and Monday evening. At least it paid the mortgage. Then I was advised to sign on in the job centre as that would open up a further range of possibilities.

The first action as a result of signing on was to be recommended for a 'Return to Nursing' course. It was held in the local hospital a mile away from my home, so I could walk or cycle there, a real bonus. Another benefit of going through the job centre was that the course was fully funded, and I received a further £17 a week, enabling me to eat. In theory anyone who went through that course would be guaranteed a nursing job at the end of it, but it was soon obvious that my chronic and serious back problems meant I would never be accepted for work on the wards. What I did gain was a better understanding of the workings of the National Health Service (NHS), and of different areas of nursing. I began to consider working as a practice nurse in a doctor's surgery.

Having sent out almost 200 letters of enquiry to all the doctors' surgeries in the area, I only received three replies, all negative. Then a response arrived from one small surgery where a husband and wife were the doctors. Their practice nurse was leaving and, following an interview, they agreed to employ me. Although I had not felt too comfortable with their ethos during the interview, there was nothing specific and there seemed no other option, so I agreed to take the job offered. They insisted that I had to supply my own uniforms and also join the Royal College of Nursing, which I did with the last of the money in the bank. Five pence kept my bank account open after spending the balance on joining the RCN and buying one uniform, and I was ready to begin work on the following Monday.

That Saturday a letter arrived from those doctors. Their nurse had decided to remain in her job, so they had cancelled the contract given to me. Several folk from the States, on their way to do some maintenance work in Lukolwe, were staying in my home for that weekend. I can remember saying out loud, as I read the letter: 'What is God trying to tell me now?'

The following Monday morning, after my visitors left, I was advised to contact the administrative body for general practitioners of the area, the Family Health Services Authority (FHSA), and to report what had happened. After speaking on the telephone, they asked me to go to the department in Harrow to discuss it all. There I learned that, having cancelled the contract in that manner, the doctors should have at least paid me a month's salary, which would have been helpful. But more than that, apparently those doctors were building up a reputation for malpractice and I was asked to put it all into writing for the FHSA's records. The overwhelming feeling I experienced was relief, as I would not have wanted to work for doctors I could not trust.

But I was still without a job!

Having returned home for lunch, the telephone rang shortly afterwards, and it was a practice manager from a general medical practice in Kingsbury, about ten miles away. They urgently needed to find someone to replace their own practice nurse, who was going on three months' maternity leave. The practice manager had followed me into the FHSA, expressed their need and been told about my experience with the other doctors. After an interview, I was accepted for the three months, stayed when their second nurse took maternity leave, a further time for the first nurse having her second baby, then job-shared with her thereafter. Having gone there for three months, I worked happily with the staff of that large health practice for more than eight years – and they supplied my uniforms!

The work proved ideal as it used much of what I had learned in the bush in Zambia, both administratively and practically. The doctors were a lovely group of people and I enjoyed working with them all. Needing a nurse to run a diabetic clinic, they sent me to study for a Diploma in Diabetic Nursing at Buckinghamshire College. Later they also financed the training for a Diploma in Asthma Care at the National Asthma Training Centre in Stratford. Thus I was able to give long-term support to our many patients suffering from either of these chronic and limiting conditions, enjoy building relationships and seeing many of them take control of their own health with new understanding. It was rewarding for the patients and for me, and a relief to the doctors to see many improving in health.

They also asked me to study the year-long specialist practice nurse diploma course, but I felt that it would not have been financially beneficial to the doctors as my working life was curtailed by age. Although I would have loved to do the course, it seemed much more sensible for them to send a younger person who could potentially give them longer service. In the end I had to leave within two years of being asked to study, for health reasons.

The part-time work at the surgery was ideal, as I was then able to spend much of the remainder of the week working as a pastoral carer with the church. It was during that time, too, that I began training as a counsellor with Waverley Abbey House (CWR). The skills learned in those courses were so valuable both for the work in the community in Northwood and also for working with the patients with long-term chronic diseases.

An interesting aspect of the whole process of finding work and signing on the 'dole', humiliating as it felt, was that pastorally, in the years to follow, I was better able to understand the experiences of other people in a similar situation. They appreciated that fact too. In some ways I had 'walked in their moccasins …'[15]

[15] 'Never criticize a man until you've walked a mile in his moccasins'; 'Great Spirit, help me never to judge another until I have walked in his moccasins.' – American Indian Proverb.
http://www.quoteland.com/author/American-Indian-Proverb-Quotes/129/ (accessed 18th July 2018).

Health

As I explained above, problems with my health were what led me to return to the UK. In the years that followed I was very thankful for the NHS as I seemed to rock from one serious medical problem to another.

In 1998 there was a lump in my breast, and the GP referred me promptly to a consultant. At the time I was reading through the Psalms. The next morning, and before that consultant's appointment, my daily reading was in Psalm 13. As I read that psalm, the words just seemed to echo what I was crying out in my heart.

> How long, O LORD? Will you forget me for ever?
> How long will you hide your face from me?
> How long must I wrestle with my thoughts
> and every day have sorrow in my heart?
> How long will my enemy triumph over me?
> Look on me and answer, O LORD my God.
> Give light to my eyes, or I will sleep in death;
> my enemy will say, 'I have overcome him,'
> and my foes will rejoice when I fall.
> But I trust in your unfailing love;
> my heart rejoices in your salvation.

I will sing to the LORD,
for he has been good to me.
(NIV 1984)

That morning I really felt as though I wrestled with
God. Then what seemed like a voice said:

'I know what is happening. I have allowed it all and I
love you and am in control. Yes, you have breast cancer,
and yes, you will have to go through all that the
treatment demands, but I will be there with you.'

As I went on meditating on that psalm, the cries of
anguish were there, but coming to verse 5 ('But I trust in
your unfailing love'), I was able to renew my trust in my
heavenly Father and rejoice in His salvation. There was
no promise of surviving the cancer, but whatever
happened, I chose to trust a trustworthy God.

But I also came away with a clear realisation that the
biggest battle was not going to be in my body, but in my
mind, and if that was under His control, it was OK. It was
a choice to trust in Him and I was able to renew my
commitment to him with the words of Psalm 19:14.

May the words of my mouth and the meditation
of my heart be pleasing in your sight, O LORD,
my Rock and my Redeemer.
(NIV 1984)

The outcome of that morning was a deep peace that
remained with me through the months and years that
followed, and also a freedom from any ongoing cry for
the Lord to heal me. He had it all under control. God was
there, He knew all about it and I could trust Him through

it all. Now I live with the fact that the cancer may break out again, not just in the near future, but at any time for the rest of my life. The same God, who revealed Himself then, is still in control and I know the freedom from anxiety that that truth brings.

An interesting aspect of that time was that just a few months earlier I had managed to completely pay off my mortgage on the house. It meant that when, during treatment, I was too unwell to return to work as a practice nurse, that responsibility had been lifted. It was also a time when the challenge of finances loomed large, and I was reminded that my heavenly Father was indeed in control. After all, He had cared and supplied throughout the twenty-five years in Zambia and would not fail now!

Following the radiotherapy I developed a chronic cough that was to plague me night and day for the next sixteen years. Then came a time when CT scanning had progressed sufficiently to show that I had a chronic lung condition called bronchiectasis, with scarring of the mucous membranes of the lungs, nose, sinuses, ears and throat. Despite trying numerous treatments, it only grew worse, to the point that the coughing spasms made it embarrassing to go out in public. Fatigue and tiredness were part of every day, and I was suffering from increasingly frequent and very severe lung infections.

Finally, in 2014, I was referred to another hospital to see a consultant in immunology. He looked through the medical history and asked a few pointed questions, and within a short time diagnosed that it was probably common variable immune deficiency (CVID) – a rare chronic immune disease which may have been present for most of my life. Tests confirmed the diagnosis and I began regular treatment with immunoglobulin. At first it was intravenous, but it soon changed to self-administered treatment weekly at home, which should continue for the rest of my life. Within months my health improved beyond belief. The cough and phlegm cleared, although I will always have the bronchiectasis and the scarring of my lungs. Energy returned, and life took on a new complexion. I was so grateful. Interestingly, since then it has been suggested that there is no way I should have survived the rigours of life in rural tropical Africa with that condition, but the One who sent me there was in control!

Two years later, a junior doctor picked up the fact that the excess calcium in my blood, causing renal colic and kidney stones from which I had suffered for more than thirty years, might be due to overgrowth of a parathyroid gland. After many tests a parathyroid adenoma (benign growth) was diagnosed and removed, with almost miraculous effect. A whole list of severe chronic symptoms suffered through the years literally vanished overnight! The biggest joy was being free of the debilitating fatigue which had drained me for so long. Of course growing older one still tires easily, but, with rest, soon recovers.

Pastoral care

Throughout this time I was involved in the local church in various ways. For more than twenty years after returning to England I had the privilege of working with others in a pastoral leadership role. As mentioned earlier, part of God's leading me from Lukolwe into a new life and work in Northwood was the new and deep desire to serve the people of this area. Once again it was amazing to realise how life and experiences, many of them in the isolation of the Zambian bush, had prepared me for that work.

Our local church has many facets of caring. A thriving mothers and toddlers group still continues today; there is also work with children of all ages, and through the years various groups have met different needs. Some have been for a certain time, or particular need or age group, and come to a natural conclusion. Others, such as the work with older folk or the Friday coffee shop, have continued for many years, and through it all there is a caring, serving group of people who reach out to others. One small group was begun many years ago by a new Christian who wanted to tell her friends and neighbours about salvation. That group, mainly women, has evolved through the years and still meets weekly for support and fellowship.

As pastoral care coordinator, it was a joy to work closely with our pastor, and we met regularly for prayer. There were numerous aspects to such pastoral work, and it gave variety and challenge to life. Providing the backup and support for those who cared for others was important, particularly as working with people can bring unexpected stresses. One example is of a lovely older couple who had a real ministry in visiting church members or others who were ill, were in hospital or had a new baby. They would take flowers, a plant or other gift, and go as our representatives. Their visits were so much appreciated. But in that work they would sometimes be discouraged, or come across issues that challenged or distressed them, and would need support. At other times a group of individuals might have found it hard working together. Spending time with them, listening and dropping 'little drops of oil' sometimes helped.

A valuable work of our church through the years has centred around food. We meet together fairly regularly for a meal as a church family, then perhaps provide meals when a family has a new baby, or at times of illness or bereavement. Home groups are very good at caring for their members too. But one area of my responsibility was to be aware of those people who might slip through the cracks, perhaps needing support in areas of life not generally known or recognised by others.

Then there were the times of crisis. It seemed that God had given me a particular gifting in that ministry. Being single and living alone meant that I was freer than most to respond to calls for help, particularly those that came at unexpected times of the day or night. Times of crisis happen in all our lives. Often we are able to cope and continue, but there are times when we need others to be there with us. This is one of the wonderful functions of the Church as a whole, to care for one another.

One of the principles by which I tried to work was to be there as support for others when they could not cope, but to be ready to step back as soon as they were able to manage again. This worked in many ways, through major and minor issues and in situations of chronic ill health.

Through the years this covered a wide range of aspects – from helping to find accommodation during homelessness, through mental health crises (sometimes involving children), to young people struggling with debt. Frequently it involved health issues, and meant enabling people to talk through their problems before going to see the doctor, visiting those in hospital (often in a practical supportive role that enabled clarification of issues between the patient and medical staff, or meeting particular needs) or accompanying someone to a consultant's appointment. Once it was babysitting some tiny children while the pastor took their mother and her other child with an injured hand to the emergency department. That stretched me!

Working with social services was sometimes encouraging, but more often frustrating. One of the special times was in a meeting of social workers, where they had openly expressed a variety of personal feelings regarding church-based work, some very negative. Then, those same people went on to declare enthusiastically that the mothers and toddlers group run at our church could not only be trusted, but was the best in the area! It was wonderful to be able to relay that news back to the hard-working, dedicated folk who led that group.

Another difficult task is in the completion of some of the application forms produced by social services. Understanding the jargon used, and what is expected by those who will receive them, is often very difficult and seems overwhelming to the people concerned. This and other skills were augmented by my attending various training courses.

Often there comes a time when it is necessary to find a place for more care for a relative or oneself. Such a search is stressful, and it is easy to make mistakes. It has often been a joy to accompany others to view care homes and find suitable accommodation. Another difficult time for any family is when a loved one is receiving terminal care. Much support is given through various services such as the Macmillan nurses, etc, but there is a special place for being able to show and share God's love as part of the church family.

As I was reading the Scriptures and talking with the Lord early one morning, I felt burdened by the thought that a particular elderly couple needed me to visit them immediately. Responding to this I went to their home and knocked on the door at 8.15am. Now, that was an unheard-of early time to disturb such people, but when the wife opened the door her first words were: 'How did you know?', and her relief was palpable. During the early hours of the morning there had been a crisis with her bedridden husband. It was possible to give them support until they were able to cope again on their own.

Some time later it was a privilege to be able to stay with them both throughout the night during which the husband went to be with the Lord he had loved and served faithfully for so many years. Then their family arrived and took over with the support needed for all the time of sadness and loss as they said goodbye.

One night, towards midnight, my phone rang. It was a mother waiting alone in the hospital Accident and Emergency to learn if her baby had meningitis. Living alone, it was easy for me to dress quickly and leave for the hospital almost immediately, giving that additional emotional support needed, and being with her as the dreaded diagnosis was made and her baby boy taken off to intensive care. Then it meant just being with her until he was well on the way to recovery.

There was a lovely but very reserved couple, not Christians. The husband developed a serious form of cancer and the pastor and I had good contact with them. One day, walking into the hospital room where he was being treated, it was to find both of them very distressed and in tears. Apparently there had been several failed attempts to insert the needle for an intravenous drip. We talked for a while and then a young doctor came in again to try to put up the drip. She quietly made several attempts before leaving the room, saying that she would be back soon. I prayed with the couple and they calmed down somewhat before the doctor returned. She too was silent and looked strained so, asking her permission, I prayed with them all for her to get the drip up and running easily. She turned around, placed the needle in the vein and had the drip running in moments. The only words she spoke were as she left the room, saying, 'Your God hears your prayers!'

But for that lovely couple it was a turning point in their lives, although I only realised it later. They had been drawn by the gospel message and the loving support they were receiving from the pastor and others and both accepted Christ as Saviour. Not long afterwards they, in their late seventies, were baptised by immersion as a statement of their new-found faith. Sometimes God performs wonders in the most unexpected places, but He knows the heart and His timing is perfect.

Eventually it was right to step down from the role of care coordinator. My health was poor and I had been able to do much less caring for others. I also needed to accept more support myself. A real joy was to know there were others who were prepared to take on the commitment. But even when we know that it is right, sometimes it is not easy to hand over to others gracefully. The timing was right, and there was a real relief at being free of the responsibilities involved, but, too, trust had grown through the years and many people, particularly some of the older folk, expressed anxiety at facing change. Through the years I had used the gifts God had given me, in sometimes unconventional ways, and that gifting was for that season. It has been wonderful to see other people led by our same heavenly Father into different aspects of pastoral work.

A new career

In the mid 1990s I took an intensive three-week counselling training course which added to the skills I needed both as a practice nurse caring particularly for people with chronic illnesses and as a pastoral worker in the local church. When I had to leave nursing, owing to my health problems, it seemed right to do more studying. So, soon after the course of radiotherapy, I began a year-long Certificate in Christian Counselling. It was hard work and physically challenging because of poor health, but also it was life-changing. Gradually I began to spend more time counselling, in addition to the pastoral work, and was amazed at how God used it to enhance people's lives. I now see a few clients each week, but am involved with people at other times too.

Young people today are taught very differently from the way we were taught in school, and that difference is clearly evidenced in tertiary education. Being thrown in at the deep end and expected to write essays to current university standards was totally different from what we used to churn out in our training days. It was a real challenge. I soon realised that I was not alone, in that many of the other counselling students were from an older generation. But, too, needing to learn different – and probably better – ways meant that I have since been able to support and help others in similar situations. This is particularly true for people from countries where English is not their primary language, and/or their schooling had been learning by rote, like so many of us.

A friend had commented that she did not see how I could be a counsellor, because I talked too much! But what surprised me even more was the way in which life in the bush in Zambia proved to have been a training ground that as a Christian counsellor gave insights and wisdom for my clients.

A few years later I went on to complete the CWR Diploma in Christian Counselling. Most of the training course for supervising counsellors was completed too, but I was unable to finish the last section of that course for health reasons. On the basis of those studies I had begun to supervise counselling students from different colleges during their initial exposure to working with clients. In 2015 I took the opportunity to repeat and complete the Diploma in Counselling Supervision. The work with students brings me great joy, particularly as they grow through that first year of exposure to actually counselling clients. So often the students start as anxious individuals who have to prove themselves, as they had to do through all the exams in school and the first year in college. Gradually they change into competent counsellors who are there for their clients. The work with students can be demanding and intensive, but very rewarding.

One experience during that last diploma course came as a surprise. As long as I could remember I had found practical actions or exams, when watched by anyone else, very difficult. I usually was unable to achieve my potential, but I thought I had learned to control my responses through the years. I did not like being watched, even when it was an area in which I knew I could do well.

During one role play session it shocked me when I froze inwardly and was unable to relate to my 'supervisee' as I desired. This left me feeling very vulnerable. Later, processing it, I was shaken to hear my mother's voice in my four-to-five-year-old head, saying, 'I will come and watch you doing ...', with my reactive dread and consequent inability to please her, even when I could accomplish that particular task with ease if not watched.

My thinking that childhood issues had all been processed years ago was challenged with these new insights. I was taken right back to the little voice that said, 'I'm not good enough', but was encouraged by the knowledge that I am, and have been, there for my supervisees. A positive outcome was the realisation that my role playing supervisee had been unaware of my inner response. But what a graphic illustration this was of how our early parental messages unconsciously drive our thoughts and behaviour. The other plus side to that insight is a deeper understanding of why and how I hide my feelings from others!

Memories

As mentioned earlier, I had very little recall of life before the age of about ten. It was some fifty years later when I woke up at two o'clock one morning, graphically remembering the circumstances that had caused me to suppress all those memories.

Not too long after we emigrated to South Africa, when I was about eight, my father lifted a weight that was too heavy for him and the retinas detached in both his eyes. A subsequent car accident on the way to hospital resulted in a fractured leg, collarbone and severe concussion, which did not help his recovery from surgery to his eyes. It was a very difficult time for my mother as we were all living in a boarding house. My father was in hospital for many months and Mum had to find someone to care for my younger brother and myself. She was out at work all day and the hospital visiting would have included considerable distances to travel.

The person she found was a young man who initially groomed me, then gradually increased the sexual abuse each evening at bedtime. He used to take us to fairgrounds and for other outings which we enjoyed, and helped my brother and myself cope with the many changes affecting our lifestyle. The abuse continued for some time, but the already deeply instilled belief that I had to cope on my own meant that there was no one to tell about it. I never told my parents. My mother was far too stressed over Dad's health and trying to work in order for us to live reasonably without his salary. I could not upset her further by making waves about the one person they had found whom they thought would safely care for us children.

At the time of recall I was doing the first year of the counselling training course and having personal counselling as part of that training. That meant I was able to talk through the traumatic issues suddenly remembered so clearly from fifty-odd years earlier, and from that day forward memories began to surface about other aspects of my childhood life, both in the UK and for the first few years in South Africa. It was as though a door had been unlocked. Uncovering those deeply buried memories meant I was able to work on understanding them. Since then it has been interesting to begin to grasp some of the long-term effects I was still experiencing as an adult – issues of trust, or why I needed to sit on the end of a row of seats, or would choose to sit where I had a wall behind me, especially in a crowded room. I recognise that the young man had robbed me of a great deal in relationships throughout my adult years, and it has been wonderful to begin to understand some of these things, forgive him and move forward.

As a child I had come to realise subconsciously that it was safer for me to be caring for others, rather than to be relating to them on a personal level. I enjoyed the relationship – perhaps when I was in control and able to walk away – but was unwilling to be vulnerable to another person. Changing schools so frequently discouraged close friendships, teaching me not to look back, but to begin anew elsewhere.

Trust had become a big issue – it was hard to trust someone completely, therefore I needed to rely on myself in order to feel safe. It was hard to accept praise, or believe others when they gave encouragement – after all, praise and encouragement had all been part of the grooming process. Later on this also affected my relationship with God to some degree, but gradually He taught me to trust Him because He is always trustworthy.

It was only many years later that I realised much of this attitude had its roots in the abuse as a child. Looking back, it shocked me to comprehend how many of my actions and reactions as an adult had been tainted by that experience. It was also emancipating in the realisation that certain incidents about which I had felt deep unnecessary shame and which I had never understood, were recognised adult reactions to such abuse. There had been two particular incidents, way back during my nursing training days, when I had struggled, at different times, to give two male patients the attention they needed. I had never understood why, but there had been deep inner struggles which left me feeling a sense of guilt and failure as a nurse. In the light of the recovered memories, it was a relief to understand the reasons for my reactions, and to forgive myself. My training as a counsellor helps my understanding too.

Another issue that affected my ability to trust others stemmed from the fact that we moved house so many times during my childhood. For me school started at age three in Keighley. Another five primary and three secondary schools later I finally left the educational system to move into an even more demanding training. By that time I had learned that one could not carry friends with one when moving on, so it seemed safer not to even make deep friendships because they would inevitably be broken. Of course, I was not conscious of this as a child, it just happened.

It was only in the years back in England that I began to process old memories and build a picture of the past. Not remembering very much about my life before the age of about ten had not really bothered me, but after the experience mentioned above, I began to remember. Then, as a result of the counselling training, I began to question the reliability of those memories ...

In 2011, a friend and I went to Dartford to explore the area where my parents had been living when I was born. It was amazing as I compared their bungalow from a photo taken in about 1939 with the present bungalow which, although extended, still shows the basic framework. Then came the most mind-boggling factor of all. I had discovered that both my grandparents had lived within five minutes' walk of our home, so I looked for their houses too. From my recently awoken memory, as my friend and I walked down the road towards the house where my maternal grandparents had lived, it was with a feeling of disappointment. True, as I thought I remembered, Dartford Heath was on the right-hand side of the road, but at each opening on to the heath I looked across and was disappointed. Not surprisingly, it did not look as it had done in my memories!

Then, as we walked around a bend … on the right, I looked across the narrow road and saw the heath exactly as I remembered it from sixty-four years before. It seemed unbelievable. There, immediately opposite my grandparents' house, was the heath on to which I had been sent out as a seven-year-old, to take care of my young brother and four younger cousins. My grandfather had just died and the adults were presumably discussing 'needful things' and we children were dispatched out of the house for many hours. My memories were of the responsibility I had been given that day, one that would not be acceptable now.

But processing the almost euphoric feelings aroused by finding it almost exactly as I remembered (almost unbelievably considering the years that had passed), I came to understand that this proved that my memories were indeed genuine. It was not something I had conjured up as a dream world of my childhood, but had actually happened. My head was spinning from the buzz of that day!

Another time when old memories were stimulated was on a visit to Keighley in Yorkshire with a friend. We found the house where our family had lived through most of the war. It was reasonably easy as I have been taught the address when very young. It was imprinted on my mind from childhood wartime days. But what I had not expected was to recognise the winding footpath leading through a farm and down to the school I had attended from ages three to seven. Although the actual school is no longer there, the path led directly to where it had been. My friend, more forthcoming than I, knocked on the door of number 5, asking if I could see inside. Although only welcomed into the kitchen, looking around I knew a door opposite us led to the cellar, although I had not even consciously remembered we had a cellar in the house. The garden appeared to have shrunk when seen from an adult point of view!

Besides the early school days in Keighley there is a strange partial memory of having my tonsils and adenoids removed, aged three. It still feels as though I was put on an ironing board (the operating table?) for the operation and was conscious of a deep fear they would start before I really went to sleep.

Thus it was that the proofs of accurate memory recall have been particularly precious, as they have shown me that the childhood memories I now enjoy are true and not just a figment of my imagination.

Relationships

I have often been asked what it is like being single or, for some cultures, why I was not married and had borne no children (in or out of marriage), as that was the only state they could understand. Now I know that it was in part because of what I have shared above. But that was accentuated by the fact that the first young man to whom I grew very close was not trustworthy. It seemed so right. He was a Bible school student in South Africa, apparently respected among Christians, yet deep down I found that I did not trust him, and sadly was later shown to be correct.

Yet singleness is a strength as well as a lonely place. Much of the work accomplished through the many years in Zambia, and even back here in the UK, might not have been possible if I had had a husband and family. I did not choose to be single, but did choose to follow what I believed was God's way for me. That meant many years of living in a very isolated place.

Through those years, from time to time, it has been necessary to lean on God in prayer and reading His Word, to enable me to lay deep inner desires at Jesus' feet and know His peace – peace that I was living in His will and plan. God made us all with a longing to love and be loved. He made us sexual beings. Emotions and the need to feel loved are built-in gifts from a loving heavenly Father, but sometimes it takes us a long time to value them fully and even longer to feel safe to express them.

Life's challenges

Hard things happen to us in the UK as well as in Africa! In about 2014 I was subjected to severe bullying. After more than twenty years of voluntarily taking responsibility for the maintenance of the grounds of our ten maisonettes, I had stepped down for health reasons. It was not an easy task and had been appreciated, particularly as no one else wanted or was free to take on the task.

After one owners' meeting one of the non-resident owners suddenly made what I considered to be unreasonable demands that involved destruction of part of my garden. When I did not immediately agree to his demands, he eventually threatened me with a lawsuit. All this seemed totally unreasonable to me. I felt distressed, falsely accused of wrongdoing and initially very angry.

Also being very ill at the time, and therefore physically weak, added to the problem. My external peace felt destroyed and the internal peace that God gives was disrupted. I was very upset and my neighbours appeared to be 'taking sides'. It was only much later that I realised that fear played a part in this. Because of various circumstances the atmosphere in our small community of ten homes had already been changing from supportive and friendly to strangers who did not interact. I just wanted to hide away. The roller coaster of emotions was difficult to control.

Taking a few days to absorb things, I then talked it over with our pastor (and he expressed anger too!). After listening, he asked the wise question, 'What do you want to pray for?', which helped to clarify my thoughts and reply:

- resolution and restoration of relationships;
- not to give in to bullying;
- to be able to genuinely forgive the person concerned.

By God's grace and in an amazing way all these were accomplished. It took time and patience. Relationships were slowly rebuilt and, for me, bitterness had gone. The whole atmosphere in this small community of diverse people has been once again restored to mutual support and caring.

Yes, I was ruffled badly – but shaken, not shattered.

> And the peace of God, which transcends all understanding, will guard your hearts and your minds in Christ Jesus.
> (Philippians 4:7)

The difficulty finding work during the early days and the story above just illustrate the fact that we, as

Christians, are in spiritual warfare wherever we live. God in His Word did not promise us an easy life. Peace is the inner strength God gives us which enables us to respond to situations as Jesus would do in our circumstances.

A new hobby

After my return to the UK, I have become fascinated with family history, and particularly that of my own family. As with so many people who emigrated in those days, contact with our extended family was lost. There were no computers, internet, mobile phones or even satellite phones. Throughout the years in Africa we had been a nuclear family of four people and I had very little consciousness of our extended family, except during that brief visit to England for the Guide World Camp in 1957. My father's brother brought his wife and son out to Rhodesia in about 1956 and, after my uncle's death in 1961, we then also had contact with my cousin, Bill, and his mother. But that was the full extent of our family.

Again it was something not questioned as a child. There were people around, acquaintances and other children, and that was life! I suppose, in many ways, many of the expatriate children who lived in southern Africa were only first or second generation and the concept of the extended family was completely foreign to them. Intercontinental transport was mainly by sea, so slow. Postal systems were minimal, and the telephone a fairly new invention that would not be used for overseas calls. International calls would have been rare, and outrageously expensive. For many years the telephone we had was a party line, where we had to turn a handle to make the various combinations of sounds that indicated the person we wanted to call. Each home on 'our' line had its own mix of short and long rings we heard in all the houses. We would listen for the rare occasion that it was our family's combination. Any conversation could be overheard by anyone else who had access to that line and picked up their receiver. As children we would never have thought of using the telephone to talk to our friends.

Thus it was that researching my family history became an enjoyable hobby, and later on I had the pleasure of using the skills I learned for other people too. Besides the fun of research on the internet, I had many wonderful holidays in Scotland following up the story.

My cousin Donald, whom I had not seen since childhood and met again during those holidays, left me a legacy which enabled me to visit his sister and her family in New Zealand. For more than fifty years it had been a deep longing of mine to visit the Milford Sound in the South Island and we enjoyed that together. The wonderful scenery through both islands was far beyond my expectations. Another particular delight was to have some time with Stuart and Anne whom I had known well in Cape Town during nursing training days. Stuart was Rose's brother, met on that first train journey from Rhodesia to Cape Town to commence nursing training! They now live north of Auckland and I had not seen them for many years. We had plenty to talk about!

Lukolwe revisited

In 2018 I had the opportunity to revisit Lukolwe and other parts of Zambia. Nicki and I flew out to Ndola, then changed to a Piper Cherokee flown by a friend to travel to Sakeji Mission School.

Some of the changes the years had wrought in Zambia were obvious – mobile phones in constant use, twenty-four-hour electricity, tarred roads and even shopping centres with a large variety of goods. But the hearts of the people were the same.

Travelling was so different. Roads that used to take us many days of hard driving are now tarred and, where the potholes are repaired, make driving clean, pleasant and quick. The small mission-based planes were in use even for taking children home from Sakeji School, and we

Image courtesy of Nicki Hunt. Used with permission.

were grateful to be flown back out from Chavuma to the Copperbelt in the Piper Cherokee.

In Zambezi township we had a tremendous welcome from the maternity nurse I worked with when first at Lukolwe more than fifty years earlier, now in her nineties. That set the pattern for the next few days. We were welcomed and remembered constantly, despite the twenty-eight years that had passed. But the best was yet to come as we spent two days at Lukolwe.

Image courtesy of Nicki Hunt.
Used with permission.

The missionary currently there came over to Chavuma to collect us in his Landcruiser and we crossed the river on the Government pontoon. A flat tyre made us feel right at home! In general, Lukolwe was as isolated and inaccessible as it had ever been. Amazingly, from the first moment I automatically spoke in fluent Luvale, with the language coming back without effort, and communication was a joy.

So many people came to greet us, some whom we had known well and others who claimed that I had delivered them or saved their lives when they were children. History is still passed down verbally among the Luvale people. Memories were fresh, stories told, and I felt so welcome and appreciated. Few people have the privilege of such joyous affirmation of their life and work. Despite the shortness of the visit, it was very special.

While we were there we learned that, among others, four men who had seemed to resist the gospel message had all come to accept Christ as Saviour – one had worked for us in our home as a young man; another as a Dresser in the hospital. A third was a political leader of the community and the fourth one of our workmen. What a joy to learn of these answers to our prayers.

Crossing the Zambezi River as we left Lukolwe.
Image courtesy of Janette Young. Used with permission.

Conclusion
Patchwork

Recently a friend of mine was busy making a patchwork quilt for her grandson. He had very specific ideas of what he wanted, and that stretched her to the limit, but the final quilt was a masterpiece. Watching her work reminded me of the many occasions when I have made patchwork quilts.

One time, when sharing with a group of ladies, we looked at how patchwork is constructed. There are so many elements of the whole – the choosing of material, planning the article, sorting out then cutting the pieces, patiently joining them together, laying out the layers that will form the quilt, then quilting the whole to give strength and durability.

Patchwork used to be done purely as a means of using scraps for clothing and to keep warm. Nowadays we see it more as a hobby than a utility, but it has always given me more satisfaction using otherwise unwanted scraps than going out and buying new material. Some time ago we made a patchwork quilt for our pastor and his wife as a memento of the love of so many friends from all over the world. Each person or family had carefully completed a 10cm square, and they were all joined together. It made a huge, beautiful quilt.

Patchwork needs careful planning and is composed of all sorts of pieces. The maker must carefully select those to be used for the process or the finished article will be neither beautiful nor strong. Sorting the good and poor patches, those of different colours, textures and durability, they then need to be put together by someone with vision and care.

Thinking about these things, it struck me that patchwork is like our lives – a collection of pieces all brought together to use. They are sourced from all the aspects of life and relationships. The patchwork of our lives was planned by a Master hand so that we could be useful to Him:

> ... instruments for special purposes, made holy, useful to the Master and prepared to do any good work.
> (2 Timothy 2:21)

As the pattern emerges through life's experiences:

- we can allow it to build in beauty ... or problems;

- we can spill dirt or stains;

- we can build in memories of joy ... or bitterness and pain.

But overall the Master's hand is at work creating and designing.

> And we know that in all things God works for
> the good of those who love him …
> (Romans 8:28)

What does this really mean to you and me? Are we 'useful to the Master'?

How can we be sure that God is working through the patterns of our lives for our good? Jesus quoted and applied to Himself the words in Isaiah. As we read it, what a mixture of ideas and purposes it is, but God had planned it all to work out into a durable and remarkable final picture:

> The Spirit of the Sovereign LORD is on me,
> because the LORD has anointed me
> to proclaim good news to the poor.
> He has sent me to bind up the broken-hearted,
> to proclaim freedom for the captives
> and release from darkness for the prisoners,
> to proclaim the year of the LORD'S favour
> and the day of vengeance of our God,
> to comfort all who mourn,
> and provide for those who grieve in Zion –
> to bestow on them a crown of beauty
> instead of ashes,
> the oil of joy
> instead of mourning,
> and a garment of praise

instead of a spirit of despair.
They will be called oaks of righteousness,
a planting of the LORD
for the display of his splendour.
(Isaiah 61:1-3)

Jesus could apply this to Himself because He saw the bigger picture. He was part of the planning stage, the One who was chosen to be the Saviour of the world.

When a person starts a piece of patchwork it is initially just little bits and pieces – it needs planning, cutting, joining, wadding, backing – and then quilting holds it all together, beautifies it and makes it durable. It is sewn with care and with a purpose in mind. A pricked finger can result in staining, but properly dealt with it can be cleansed, yet sometimes leaves traces of the mark as a reminder!

> My life is just a weaving between my God and me;
> I do not see the colors He worketh steadily.
> Oft'times He weaveth sorrow and I, in foolish pride,
> Forget He sees the upper and I the underside.
>
> Not 'til the loom is silent and the shuttles cease to fly,
> will God unroll the canvas and explain the reason why.

The dark threads are as needful in the skilful
weaver's hand
As the threads of gold and silver in the pattern
He has planned.[16]

We cannot know this for certain unless we have a personal individual relationship with God. God, Himself, has said that there is only one way to that relationship and it is through His Son, Jesus (see John 14:6).

Looking back on the years of childhood, then Lukolwe and now the further years here in the UK, it still makes me marvel that a loving heavenly Father planned and executed so many things during my life, in preparation for the work He had for me in the years that were to follow. Although seldom recognised at the time, there in the isolated places He taught through joys and my failures, through hard times, the indescribable wonder of seeing Him at work and His provision for every need.

'For I know the plans I have for you,' declares
the LORD ...
(Jeremiah 29:11)

---

[16] Author unknown. See http://www.theworshipbook.com/blog/lyrics-whodunnit (accessed 1st May 2018).

Appendix 1
More cross-cultural issues

In October 1990, after my return to the UK, I was on the editorial committee for *Footsteps* magazine, a Tearfund production devoted to health, medical and basic issues to promote healthy living, particularly in rural areas of the world. I replied to one letter received regarding traditional cultural issues and I will share some of it here, as it shows clearly other areas of learning in new cultures. The article was published in *Footsteps* 8, in September 1991, and went on to use the principles suggested to respond to the writer of the letter.

When we move into a difficult cultural situation and begin to understand people's beliefs in health or other areas, we often face difficulties in teaching new ideas.

Perhaps one of the first principles to remember is that there is much good in every culture, and simply because something is different from our ways it is not necessarily wrong. We need to understand people's beliefs thoroughly and then to build upon them to bring meaningful change.

Cultural beliefs can be divided into ...

- helpful;
- harmful;
- neither helpful or harmful.

Take time to assess each belief with these criteria. This can be very helpful in working out our response to that belief and the actions resulting from it. We need to work from where the people are – from the very basis of their beliefs and traditions. It may take many months, even years, to understand what lies behind some beliefs, but without this understanding it may be impossible to improve the whole situation.

Sit and take time to talk with people of all ages and understand the basis of their beliefs.

Case study

In the area of Zambia in which I worked, there was the belief that if a mother became pregnant again before the previous baby was actually walking, then the breast milk turned bad and the first baby would die. This resulted in a cultural taboo on sex for the mother before that child was walking, and also a speedy weaning of such a child if the mother should become pregnant. Then the child would weaken and often die, usually from malnutrition and infection, as a result of poor weaning foods and complete lack of milk intake – so the belief was carried on.

The older women ('grandmothers') encouraged the belief, both because they believed it to be fact, and because they wanted to encourage traditional practices in the younger generation – a weaned child would often go to live with grandmother (which pleased her).

The younger women longed for another view that would 'liberate' them – the belief created stress in monogamous marriages and often resulted in infidelity, or the resort to polygamy to fill the gap.

Helpful aspects

- A twenty-one-month gap (or longer) between births was good for the mother's health.

- The baby received the mother's full attention for at least twenty-one months.

- Breast feeding for more than eighteen months was very good for the baby.

Harmful aspects

- The mother's fear that her breast milk would poison the baby.

- The fantastic attitude that the child would die and it would be her fault.

- The 'justified' infidelity and polygamy.

In this situation, the positive aspects needed to be encouraged without strengthening all that the 'grandmothers' said. They were the key people. But the role of the men was important. The younger men were used to recognising the truths learned through education and could have an active role in change. The younger couples were often moving out of the cultural society of their parents (by urbanisation, education, etc). If the men would accept changes, they strongly influenced their wives.

Appropriate responses

1. Support of those few mothers who became pregnant before the older child was walking, encouraging them to continue breastfeeding as long as possible.

2. Providing a viable alternative method of family planning.

3. Health teaching – on the use of locally available weaning foods and the value of breast milk even if a mother became pregnant again – was given:

- on an individual basis to the distressed mother;

- to all mothers at antenatal clinics and visits;

- in the home environment and in ways and language acceptable for the older women;

- to the husband and other men of the community;

- to schoolchildren, who often care for their younger siblings and will soon be parents themselves.

If traditional beliefs are ...

Helpful: Encourage them.

Harmful: Identify the root of the problem. Seek some non-offensive means of change. Start from where they are now.

Neither: Ignore them.